Picture-Perfect
Origami

Picture-Perfect Origami

All you need to know to make fantastic
origami creations shown in step-by-step photos

Nick Robinson

St. Martin's Griffin
New York

A QUARTO BOOK

ORIGAMI BASICS
For information, address
St. Martin's Press, 175 Fifth Avenue,
New York, N.Y. 10010.

www.stmartins.com

Library of Congress Cataloging-in-Publication
Data is available upon request

ISBN-13: 978-0-312-37596-6
ISBN-10: 0-312-37596-4

First U.S. Edition: March 2008

Conceived, designed, and produced by
Quarto Publishing plc
The Old Brewery
6 Blundell Street
London N7 9BH

QUA: ORB

Editor: Michelle Pickering
Art director: Caroline Guest
Art editor: Natasha Montgomery
Designer: James Lawrence
Photographers: Simon Pask, Phil Wilkins

Creative director: Moira Clinch
Publisher: Paul Carslake

Color separation by Provision (PTE) Ltd,
Singapore
Printed by 1010 Printing International Ltd,
China

10 9 8 7 6 5 4 3 2 1

Contents

Introduction   6

CHAPTER 1:
Getting Started   **8**
Paper   10
Preparation   12
Techniques   14
Bases   26

CHAPTER 2:

Simple Designs   32

Wingding	34
Penguin	37
Sailboat	40
Fortune-teller	42
Basketball hoop	46
Banger	50
Finger puppet	53
Jaws 1	56
Crown	60
Star box	64
Tulip	68
Waterbomb	72
Butterfly	76
Sanbow	
(Box with legs)	80
Ninja star	84

CHAPTER 3:

Contemporary Designs   90

Gift box	92
Jaws 2	94
Modular cube	96
Narrow box	98
Face lift	100
T-Rex	102
Mouse behind cheese	104
Wentworth bowl	106
Pipe	108
Locked box	110
Boat with keel	112
Wild goat	114
Sentinel bird	116
Skunk	118
Around the houses	120
Welsh corgi	123

Index	126
Credits	128

Introduction

Origami is the Japanese word for paper folding. Origami dates back many hundreds of years in Japan, but in the last 60 years or so it has developed into a widespread creative art practiced all around the world. The reasons for this are threefold. First, a small group of dedicated individuals worked tirelessly to "spread the word" and build networks of folders, leading to the formation of origami societies. Second, an increasing number of books on the subject, with standards of illustration that have risen rapidly over the years, have helped novice folders to achieve success in their folding efforts. Third and most recently, the internet has made origami accessible to anyone in the world with just a few clicks of a mouse. There are thousands of diagrams you can print out and technical help of all kinds is available from the many origami society websites.

From one viewpoint, paper folding is a solitary hobby, in which you, the instructions, and a sheet of paper combine to produce a small piece of paper art. Without this dedication and desire for mastery, it is unlikely that you will progress far. However, origami can also be a very sociable group activity. In most countries, small groups of folders living close to each other will gather for regular meetings, to help each other through folding problems, to share books, and to enthuse about new designs. Keen paper folders also travel around the world to attend annual origami conventions and to display their latest creations. Once again, the internet makes the organization of such excursions relatively simple.

Like any serious art or craft, the basics of the subject are simple, but it can take a lifetime to master them. This book is intended to start you on that path, and while the basics are covered, some of the later designs will reveal unexpected subtleties in technique and folding sequence. If you are new to the subject, you are strongly advised to work through the designs in sequence and to fold and unfold each one many times, until you understand not only how to make the design, but also how the creases and folds combine to produce the finished model. The better your understanding of the basics, the more beautiful your folds will be and you will be able to progress to the next level.

Getting Started

This chapter introduces the basic techniques needed to create

the models in this book and those you may find on the internet

or elsewhere. You can skip past this section and start folding

models straight away, but inevitably, you will need to return and

look up specific techniques. The "language" of origami diagrams

is surprisingly simple—part of the appeal of origami is seeing what

complexity can be produced with the use of simple elements.

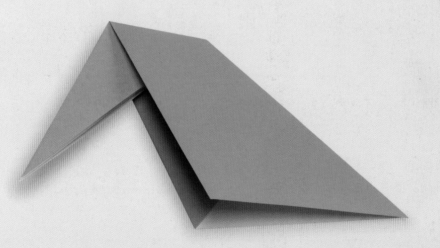

Paper

There are many types of paper, each of which has a slightly different composition. Some are suitable for folding (they will "remember" the crease), while others are not. Try folding everything you can find and you will soon learn to recognize "good" paper. Build up a collection of different colors and patterns, so that you can choose a suitable paper for a given subject. Proper origami paper can be bought and is not usually too expensive, but you can fold many other types of paper. Here are some widely available paper types you should experiment with.

ORIGAMI PAPER

This is perfectly square (or should be) and comes in a huge variety of colors and patterns, as well as several different sizes. Typical origami paper, known as "kami" paper, is white on one side and colored on the other. However, you can also buy paper that has different colors on either side, perfect for decorative designs that reveal both sides of the paper.

PHOTOCOPY PAPER

This comes in a variety of colors and is inexpensive, so it is perfect for practicing with. The only snag is that it is rectangular, so you will need to cut it down to a square shape for most designs.

WRAPPING PAPER

Ordinary brown wrapping paper (sometimes known as "kraft" paper) has excellent folding properties and has the added advantage of focusing attention on the model rather than on the paper itself. It is often sold in large rolls that can then be cut down to size. Other types of colorful gift-wrapping paper can also be used, but avoid plastic-based gift wrap because it is unsuitable for folding.

FOIL PAPER

This has one shiny metallic side and one plain white side. It is not the best material for beginners, because it is very difficult to change crease directions. The origami community is divided about foil—some love it, others hate it.

FINE-ART PAPER

This is slightly thicker and more expensive than other types of paper, but it has a texture and strength that give models a quality finish. It is also perfect for the technique of "wet folding," whereby you dampen the paper before folding; when the paper dries, it keeps its shape perfectly.

PAPER MONEY

Any simple design that starts with a rectangular sheet can usually be made from paper money. It is also strong and long-lasting, although it can obviously be an expensive folding material.

FOUND PAPER

You can fold with almost any type of paper, so don't overlook the free supplies available in most stores, at advertising events, and with products—leaflets, posters, paper bags, tickets, handouts, and so on. Much of it is low-grade, but still fine for making simple designs.

Preparation

You should always apply the highest standards to your folding, taking as much time as necessary to make every crease as perfect as possible. The first few times you make a model, it may not look wonderful—you should fold it again and again, trying each time to improve on the last effort. Practice folding and creasing different types of paper to get a feel for their different qualities.

POSITIONING AND CREASING

Make sure the appropriate edges or corners meet perfectly before creasing the paper, because once a crease is made, you cannot make it disappear. You may find it is easier to make some folds if you move the paper to a different position from that shown in the instruction. You should do anything that makes folding easier and more accurate, but remember to put the paper back in its original position afterward, so that it matches the next drawing in the instructions before continuing.

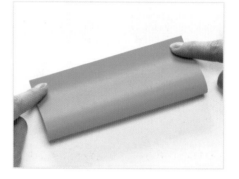

1 Fold the paper as indicated in the instruction. Check the position of the fold carefully. In most cases, it is easiest to fold paper away from you so that you can see the edge you are creasing.

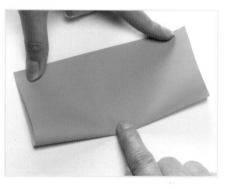

2 When you are happy with the fold, use the fingers of one hand to hold the paper firmly in place, spreading your fingers as much as possible. Place a finger of your other at the center of the folded edge.

3 Start the crease by sweeping your finger along the fold to one side.

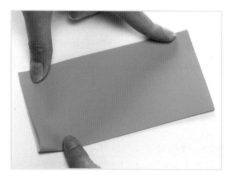

4 Continuing to hold the paper steady with your other hand, sweep your finger to the other side.

5 Use a finger from either hand to reinforce the crease. To start with, always make every crease as sharp as you can.

USING A FOLDING BONE

Although it is not really necessary, some folders use a tool, called a folding bone, to reinforce their creases. Made from bone or plastic, it has a hard edge to make firm creases.

CUTTING PAPER TO SIZE

All the models in this book start with either a square or rectangle of paper. Depending on the type of paper you are using, you may need to cut it to shape. If you have a spare piece of paper, make a square or rectangle from that and use it as a template to cut another piece of paper. This will avoid getting unwanted creases in the design.

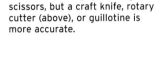

You can cut the paper using scissors, but a craft knife, rotary cutter (above), or guillotine is more accurate.

Cutting a square from a rectangle

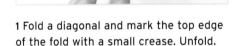

1 Fold a diagonal and mark the top edge of the fold with a small crease. Unfold.

2 Fold over the edge of the paper at the crease mark. Crease the whole fold.

3 Unfold and cut off the end of the paper to leave a square.

Cutting a rectangle from a square

1 Fold a square in half diagonally, then fold one side to lie along the crease. Pinch where the edge folds.

2 Unfold, then fold the opposite side edge so that it meets the pinch mark, aligning the edges neatly. Crease firmly.

3 Unfold and cut off the end of the paper. This will leave a rectangle of roughly letter-size (A4) proportions.

FOLDING TIPS

- Always use a firm, flat surface to fold on, such as a desk or table. More experienced folders are able to fold in midair, but it adds greatly to the difficulty. Make sure you have "elbow room."
- Try to fold under the right conditions—clear a table, make sure there is plenty of light, and choose a time when you will not be interrupted and can concentrate.
- If you do struggle, try folding with a few friends so that you can help each other through tricky steps.
- There are thousands of websites with hints, tips, and diagrams for you to try. If you want, you can also join an origami society—there is usually one in every country.

Techniques

Here are the basic techniques you will need to complete the designs in this book. You should practice these with scrap paper until you understand them fully. Try altering angles and distances to see how it affects the result. No matter how complex they are, all origami designs are made up from these simple sequences. As with playing a musical instrument, mastering the basics is the only way you will progress to more complex designs.

VALLEY FOLD

This is the simplest origami fold. It involves folding the paper and creasing it in the same way that you would fold a letter.

Instruction

Valley fold

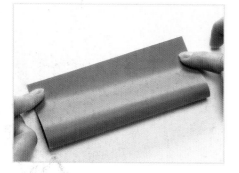

1 Arrange the paper so that you are folding away from yourself. Holding the edge with both hands, fold the paper into exactly the right position.

2 Use one hand to hold the paper firmly in the proper position, then use the first finger of the other hand to start the crease in the center of the folded edge.

3 Press the finger along the edge, working outward to either side.

4 When the crease is completed, use a finger from each hand to reinforce it, working from the center out.

ORIGAMI SYMBOLS

Origami diagrams use a standard set of symbols to provide all the basic information you need to complete a model.

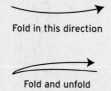 Fold in this direction

 Repeat once

 Fold point to point

 Fold and unfold

 Repeat twice

 Fold behind

Fold and unfold

 Repeat three times

 Pleat fold

MOUNTAIN FOLD

This is the opposite of the valley fold—if you make a valley fold and then turn the paper over, you will have a mountain fold.

Instruction

Mountain fold

1 In most cases it is easiest to turn the paper over and make a valley fold.

2 Crease firmly, then turn the paper to the correct position afterward to match the diagrams.

CHANGING CREASE DIRECTION

From time to time you will be asked to convert a crease from valley to mountain, or vice versa. This means that the crease line already exists—it is "precreased." Once the fibers of wood in the paper have been creased, it is easy to swap them around. Simply swing the paper around to the opposite side.

LOCATION CREASE OR PINCH

Sometimes you will need to make a fold that does not line up with an edge or corner. To do this, create a small crease, sometimes referred to as a location crease or pinch. For example, you may need to fold to the center of a square, but without making too many unnecessary creases.

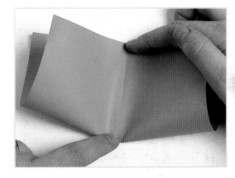

Align the paper as required, then pinch a very small, gentle crease.

Location crease

Turn over

Rotate 90 degrees

Rotate 180 degrees

Push or press

Pull out paper

Inflate

Enlarged view

Equal distances

— — — — —
Valley fold

— · — · — ·
Mountain fold

· · · · · · · · ·
Hidden fold

_____
Existing crease

FOLD AND UNFOLD

A double-headed arrow means you should crease and then unfold the paper. Alternatively, a single arrow may indicate where the fold starts from and returns to.

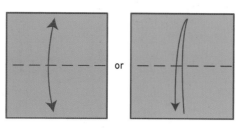

Instructions

1 Fold the paper as indicated. If you need to rotate the paper to make the fold easier, that's fine, but return it to its original position afterward so that it matches the next diagram.

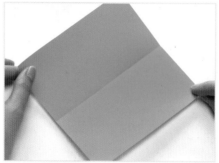

2 Unfold the paper and continue as instructed.

CHANGING ORIENTATION

With many steps, life is made easier if you alter the position of the paper. You should do this whenever it helps. Sometimes an instruction will specifically indicate that you should turn the paper over or rotate it to a new position. Whenever you see the "turn over" arrow, turn the paper over in the direction the arrow is pointing. The rotation symbol indicates that you should rotate the paper, usually by 90 or 180 degrees—the length of the arrow indicates this. You can also tell by looking at the next drawing.

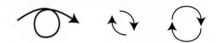

Turn paper over   Rotate 90º   Rotate 180º

REPEAT FOLD

If an arrow, whether single- or double-headed, has a small line (or lines) across it, it means you should repeat the fold somehow. This generally means repeating the move on the opposite side of the paper—most origami designs are symmetrical. If a repeat arrow has three lines on it, you will be repeating three times, such as folding four corners into the center. The symbol is used to reduce the number of diagrams needed to explain a model. This example demonstrates a single repeat.

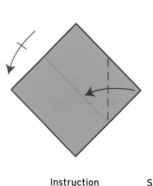

Instruction

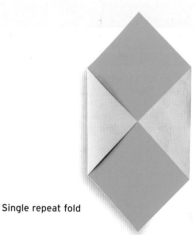

Single repeat fold

1 Start with a square, folded in half from side to side. Rotate the paper if necessary to make folding easier.

2 Unfold, then fold one corner into the center of the paper, using the diagonal crease to align it accurately.

3 Repeat with the opposite corner.

PLEAT

A pleat is simply a combination of a mountain and a valley fold. The order in which you make the folds is up to you—whatever is easiest.

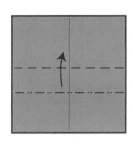

Instruction

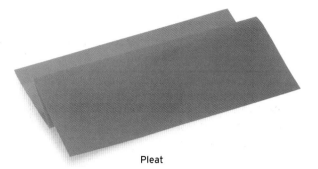

Pleat

1 Position the paper as required, then make the first crease. Here, the mountain fold is being made first.

2 Turn over and rotate the paper so that it is in the correct position to make the second crease of the pleat.

3 Make the valley crease to complete the pleat.

FOLD POINT TO POINT

Many origami moves involve aligning edges, but not all. Sometimes you will need to take a corner or point on an edge and fold it to another given point. The general principle is to treat it as a normal valley fold, but be extra careful to position the paper as indicated. If the location point is not obvious, you may see a small circle or dot to show the position.

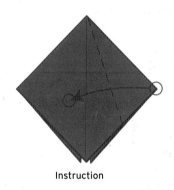

Instruction

Carefully identify the start and end point of the fold, then make the fold.

Folded point to point

SCALE INCREASES

As the paper is folded, it generally becomes smaller. To avoid the diagrams doing the same, from time to time the drawings are enlarged. An arrow is sometimes used to indicate this, although you may not even notice that it has happened.

FOLD EQUAL AMOUNTS

Often at the start of a model, you will be instructed to fold the paper into equal quarters or thirds. The sequence for this may be shown, or the "fold equal amounts" symbol used. You can then decide for yourself how to achieve it. Folding into quarters is simple to do (fold the paper in half, then fold each half in toward the center fold), but folding into thirds is more tricky.

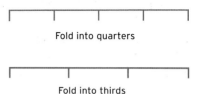

Fold into quarters

Fold into thirds

Folding into thirds

In some cases, you can use your judgment to fold thirds. However, most of the time the division needs to be accurate. There are a number of ways of doing this, all of which add unwanted creases to the paper. Make these creases very lightly, as you would a location crease.

1 Start with a square that has been creased in half vertically. Starting at the lower left corner, fold the lower right corner up so that it lies on the vertical center crease. Don't flatten the paper; simply position it.

2 Pinch the paper to make a tiny crease at the lower end of the vertical crease, then unfold.

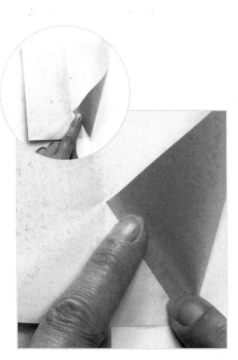

3 Fold the lower right corner to meet the pinch mark, again without flattening the paper. Make a tiny crease at the lower edge, then unfold.

4 This pinch mark is one third of the distance along the lower edge from the right corner. Fold the lower left corner to meet it to add a one-third crease in the left-hand section of the paper.

5 Fold the right edge of the paper over to the crease you have just made to divide the paper into equal thirds.

Creating thirds from a template

You can avoid unwanted creases altogether by marking accurate thirds on one square of paper, and then using this as a template to add third creases neatly onto another square.

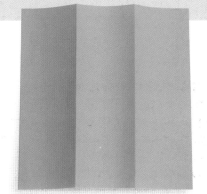

Thirds using folds   Thirds using a template

1 On the template sheet of paper, mark out and fold one third of the paper over, as demonstrated in steps 1–4 on page 18.

2 Place the template on top of the paper you wish to fold, lining up the top corners.

3 Hold firmly and fold the lower sheet over the template.

4 Crease firmly, starting in the center and working out to each side.

5 Separate the sheets and discard the template. Fold the opposite edge of the remaining paper over to the third crease you have just made.

6 Crease firmly, then unfold. You will see that you have creased the paper into accurate thirds, with no unnecessary crease marks.

REVERSE FOLDING

This involves changing (reversing) the direction of the creases from valley to mountain or vice versa, so that you can wrap part of the paper around the outside or to the inside. Reverse folding is always made easier by precreasing. A kite base (see page 26) is used as the starting point for these demonstrations.

Instruction

Outside reverse fold

Outside reverse fold

1 Fold the kite base in half.

2 Make a precrease to mark the position of the reverse fold. Unfold.

3 Open the paper slightly and wrap the layer around the outside. This will reverse all of the precreases.

Inside reverse fold

The black triangle indicates the direction in which you should apply pressure when forming the reverse fold.

Instruction

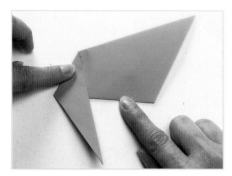

1 Start with a kite base folded in half, as before. Make a precrease to position the reverse fold, then unfold.

2 Open the paper slightly and gently push the flap inside the original layers, reversing the precreases on both sides as you do so.

Inside reverse fold

Double reverse fold

This is simply a combination of an inside and an outside reverse fold. It is often used for creating heads and beaks.

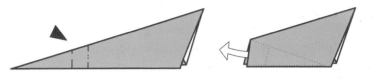

Instructions

1 Start with a kite base folded in half.

2 Form a pleat to mark the position of the reverses, then unfold.

3 Sink the whole point inside the layers, at the farthest crease from the point.

4 Use a finger to apply pressure to the crease nearest the point, and at the same time pull the point of the paper back out. Neaten all the folds.

Double reverse fold

PULL PAPER OUT

A hollow or white arrow indicates that paper (a flap or perhaps a layer) is to be eased out from wherever it lies.

CRIMP

A crimp is a type of pleat that allows you to create a change of angle in a strip or pointed flap. The paper that is "lost" in the fold lies either inside or outside the rest of the paper, determining whether it is an inside or outside crimp. A crimp acts like a hinge, and is often used when forming heads. In this example, start with a square of paper folded in half.

Instruction

Inside crimp

Inside crimp

1 Precrease the first indicated crease through both layers (here, the vertical crease is being made).

2 Precrease the second indicated crease through both layers (here, the diagonal crease). Open out the paper.

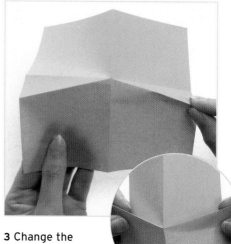

3 Change the direction of the creases to valley and mountain folds, as indicated, on both sides. Refold in half.

Outside crimp

1 Precrease both indicated creases through both layers, in the same way as when forming an inside crimp.

2 Change the direction of the creases to mountain and valley folds in the correct order, so that this time the paper swivels on the outside rather than the inside.

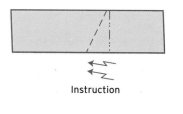
Instruction

Outside crimp

RABBIT'S EAR

This is so named because the central triangular flap that is formed looks a bit like an ear (but not really like a rabbit's ear). Here, you see the classic form of this technique, but the angles can be adapted.

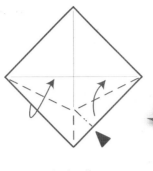

Instruction

Rabbit's ear

1 Start with a square that has been folded along both diagonals.

2 Fold the lower left edge up to the horizontal diagonal.

3 Crease from the corner as far as the center vertical crease.

4 Unfold, then repeat step 3 with the lower right edge.

5 Fold both sides in at the same time, making a small valley fold along the center vertical crease. Both sides should meet in the center to form a vertical flap, known as a rabbit's ear.

6 Fold the rabbit's ear to one side.

SQUASH

Whenever you have two edges joined at one end, you can squash that point. The squash is usually symmetrical, but may not always be so. As with most origami moves, if you take care to make accurate precreases, it will happen quite easily.

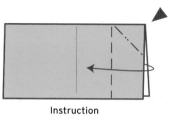

Instruction

1 Start with a square. Crease it in half vertically, then unfold. Crease it in half horizontally, and leave it folded.

2 Fold a short edge to the center, crease, and unfold. Rotate the paper so the fold is toward you to make folding easier and more accurate.

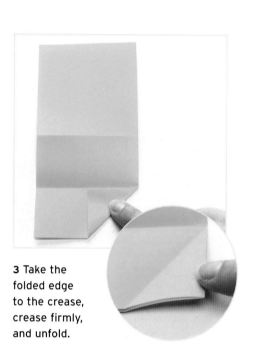

3 Take the folded edge to the crease, crease firmly, and unfold.

4 Fold the upper layer over on the crease you made in step 2, taking the edge up to the center horizontal crease. The folded edge at the corner will start to open out and move down.

5 Keep pressing the end of the flap so that it spreads into a triangle. Crease the squash fold firmly.

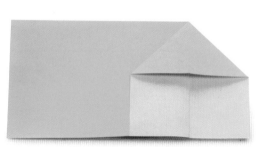

Squash

SINK

Sometimes a folding sequence creates a folded point that you don't want. Rather than cutting it off, you can sink it out of the way. The easiest method is to use an open sink, which involves opening out the paper and arranging the creases so that you can sink the point inside. A closed sink involves applying pressure to the point so that it "pops" inside, without opening out the paper. In this demonstration, the point of a waterbomb base (see page 30) is hidden with an open sink.

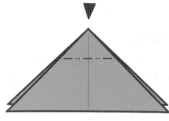

Instruction

1 Starting with a waterbomb base, fold the point over to create the sinking point and crease very firmly. Some people recommend creasing it back and forth (valley and mountain) to reinforce the crease, but this is not necessary.

2 Open the paper and alter the sink creases around the edge to be mountain folds. This will form a small square.

3 Press in the center and start to form diagonal valley folds within the square.

4 Keep pressing the edges together until the point is fully sunk.

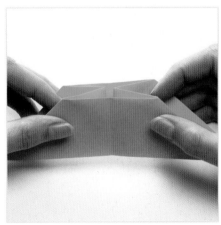

5 Flatten the paper to complete the sink fold.

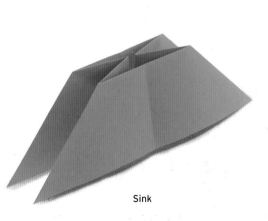

Sink

Bases

These are sequences of folds that are used to start many models. Since they are used so often, they have been given names to identify them, allowing us to skip several steps of a diagrammatic sequence by saying, for example, "start with a kite base." You should learn these by heart, because they occur in thousands of different models. The bases demonstrated here are used for the models in this book, and you will find diagrammatic reminders whenever they are used for the simple designs in Chapter 2. You will come across others as you continue to explore origami, as well as different methods of folding the bases.

KITE BASE
Using only three creases, the kite base is the simplest of all the traditional bases.

1 Start with a square, white side up. Fold in half diagonally, crease, and unfold.

2 Fold one side to lie along the diagonal crease.

3 Fold the other side to lie along the diagonal crease. This completes the kite base.

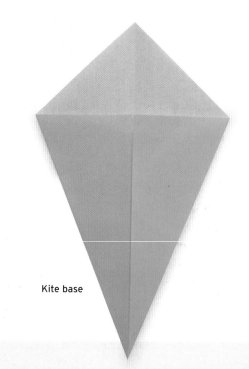

Kite base

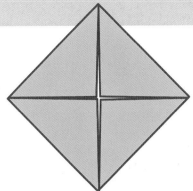

BLINTZ BASE

This a simple base that takes its name from a Jewish pastry technique. Because you are folding four corners to the center, you need know where the center is. You can do this either by folding diagonally both ways, or side to side one way.

Method 1

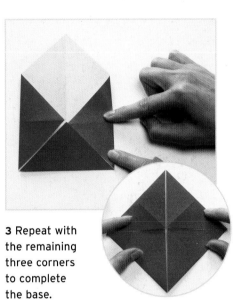

1 Start with a square, white side up. Fold in half diagonally in both directions. Crease and unfold.

2 Fold one corner to the center of the square, aligning the point carefully.

3 Repeat with the remaining three corners to complete the base.

Method 2

1 Start with a square, white side up. Fold in half horizontally. Fold the two shorter edges up to meet the horizontal crease.

2 Turn the paper over and repeat on the other side.

3 Unfold the horizontal crease to reveal the completed base.

Try it out

Crown, page 60
Sanbow (Box with legs), page 80
Wentworth bowl, page 106

Blintz bases

PRELIMINARY BASE
This is named because it is preliminary to many traditional designs. It consists simply of creases from corner to corner and side to side.

1 Start with a square, colored side up. Crease in half diagonally.

2 Unfold, then repeat along the other diagonal. Unfold again.

3 Turn the paper over and crease in half from side to side. Unfold.

4 Rotate the paper 90 degrees and crease in half from side to side again, so that you now have vertical, horizontal, and diagonal creases.

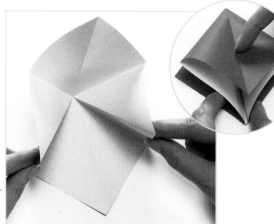

5 Rotate the paper so that a corner is toward you, then use the creases to bring the top corner toward you as well. The side points will fold inward as you do so.

Try it out
Star box, page 64

Preliminary base

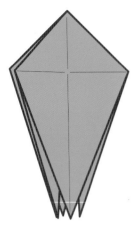

BIRD BASE

This base is perhaps best known as the base from which the flapping bird and the traditional crane are made, but it has been used to make other birds and many different subjects. Start with a preliminary base (see page 28), colored side outward and with the corners of the original square at the bottom.

1 Fold the raw edges of the uppermost layer to the vertical center crease.

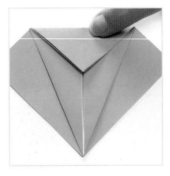

2 Fold the top triangular section down over these two flaps.

3 Unfold the two flaps from beneath the triangle.

4 Lift the uppermost layer by the bottom point and swing it upward. The outside flaps will begin to fold inward.

5 Allow the paper to flatten and crease the folds firmly. This technique is called "petal folding."

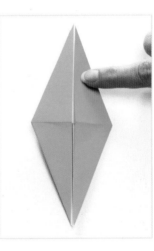

6 Turn the paper over and repeat on the other side.

7 Fold the upper flap downward, then repeat on the other side to complete the base.

Try it out
Sentinel bird, page 116

Bird base

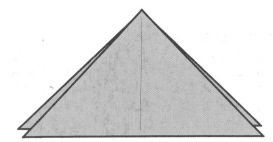

WATERBOMB BASE

This is named after a schoolchildren's design called the waterbomb, which starts with this sequence. It is in fact the preliminary base turned inside out—try it and see.

1 Start with a square, colored side up. Crease side to side both ways.

2 Turn the paper over and crease diagonally.

3 Repeat with the other diagonal.

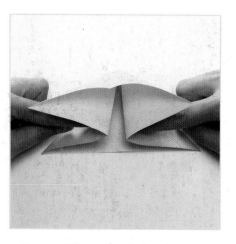

4 Open out the paper and position it so that one straight edge is toward you. Use the creases to bring the top corners toward you, pressing your fingers along the horizontal center crease to bring in the sides.

5 The upper edge will fold down to complete the base. Reinforce the creases.

Try it out

Basketball hoop, page 46
Tulip, page 68
Waterbomb, page 72
Boat with keel, page 112

Waterbomb
base

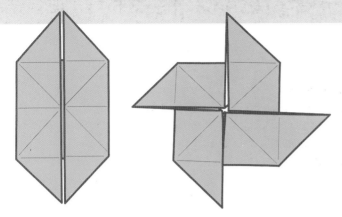

MULTIFORM AND WINDMILL BASES

The multiform base is very flexible and can be used to create many models. When arranged in a pinwheel design, it is known as the windmill base. There are several ways to fold these bases; this one is the most direct, and starts with an unfolded waterbomb base (see page 30).

1 Unfold the waterbomb base so that the mountain diagonals are upward.

2 Fold each corner to the center, crease, and unfold.

3 Turn the paper over and fold each side to the center. Crease and unfold.

4 Start to fold the halfway points of each side in toward the center. You do not need any extra creases.

5 When these points are at the center, flatten two triangular flaps toward the top and two toward the bottom. This forms a multiform base.

6 Swing two of the flaps in the other direction to form a windmill base.

Try it out
Butterfly, page 76
Modular cube, page 96

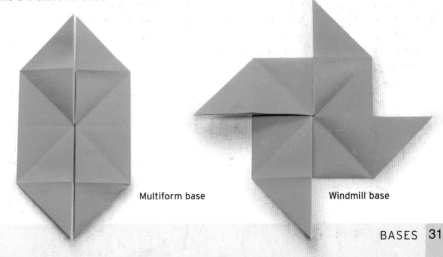

Multiform base

Windmill base

Simple Designs

This chapter contains a selection of designs, both traditional and original, chosen for their simplicity and for the techniques needed to complete them. Follow the step-by-step diagrams carefully, referring to the accompanying hands-on photographs for clarification. When you have finished each step, compare your work to the photographs in the colored panel at the bottom of the pages. These show exactly what the model should look like at the end of each step, so you can check that you are folding it correctly.

Wingding

This is a classic example of an "action" model—one that does something when completed. There are many "flapping" origami designs and they never fail to delight. This one is by Florence Temko of the United States. She has written dozens of craft books over the last 30 years and is still active both writing about and creating origami. She loves simple designs that anyone can fold, so this one is ideal for beginners.

MAKING THE WINGDING

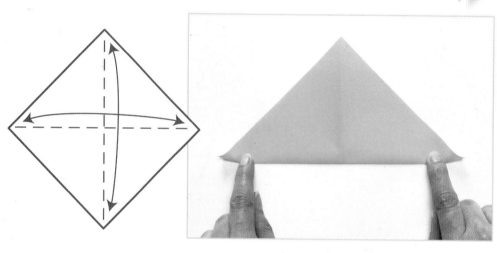

▲ **1** Start with a square, white side up. Valley fold (see page 14) both diagonals, crease, and unfold.

▲ **2** Fold the lower left edge to the horizontal crease. Crease and unfold.

→ **WATCH THE MODEL FOLD UP...**

1 Crease diagonally

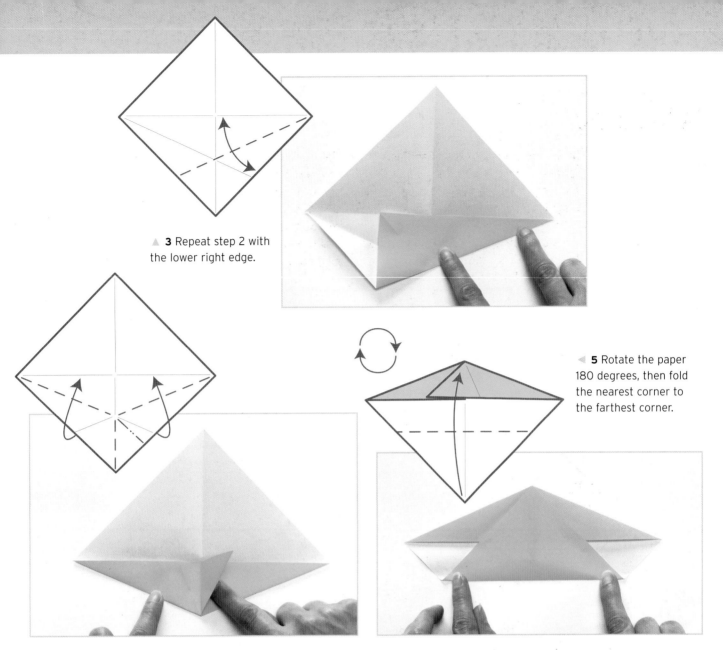

▲ **3** Repeat step 2 with the lower right edge.

▲ **4** Form a rabbit's ear (see page 23).

◀ **5** Rotate the paper 180 degrees, then fold the nearest corner to the farthest corner.

2 Crease the lower left edge

3 Crease the lower right edge

4 Form a rabbit's ear

5 Rotate and fold up the bottom corner

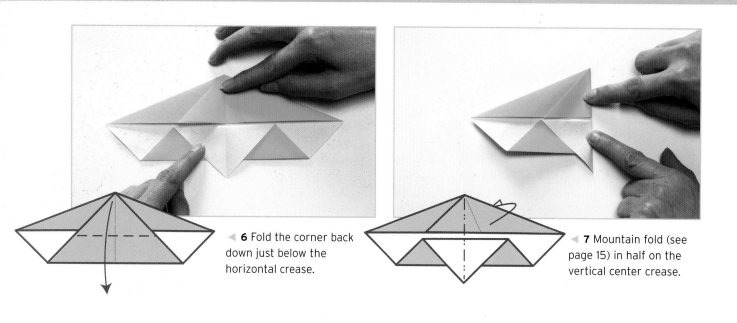

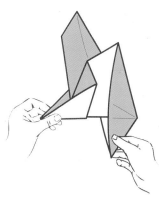

6 Fold the corner back down just below the horizontal crease.

7 Mountain fold (see page 15) in half on the vertical center crease.

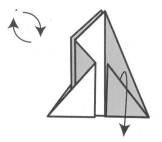

8 Rotate to this position and fold down the flap on the right.

9 Hold where shown and ease your hands apart to make the model flap.

6 Fold the top point down (photos now enlarged for clarity)

7 Fold in half

8 & 9 Rotate, fold down the right flap, then flap the wings

Penguin

This traditional model is perfect for beginners, because none of the folds needs to be precise, except perhaps for making the initial base. The way the head is brought out in step 9 can be achieved by making an outside reverse fold (see page 20) directly into the paper if you prefer. Although all origami consists of separate folding steps, there are many ways in which a sequence can be varied and yet still produce the same result.

KITE BASE REMINDER

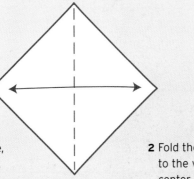

1 Start with a square, white side up. Fold, crease, and unfold one diagonal.

2 Fold the lower edges to the vertical center crease.

3 The completed kite base (see page 26).

MAKING THE PENGUIN

1 Start with a kite base (see above).

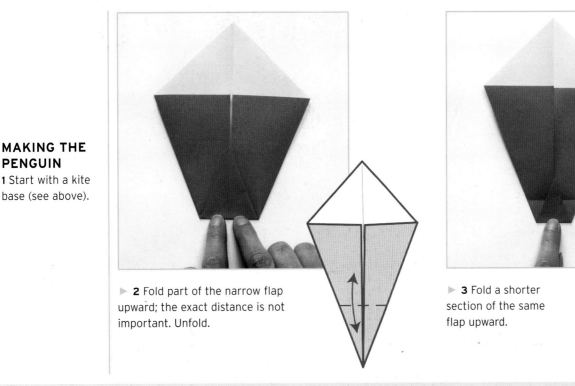

▶ **2** Fold part of the narrow flap upward; the exact distance is not important. Unfold.

▶ **3** Fold a shorter section of the same flap upward.

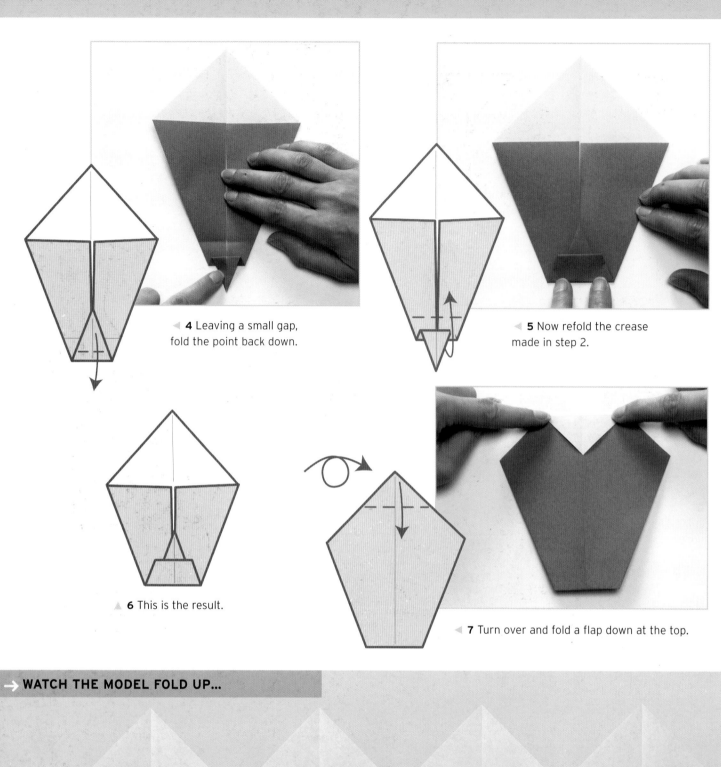

◀ **4** Leaving a small gap, fold the point back down.

◀ **5** Now refold the crease made in step 2.

▲ **6** This is the result.

◀ **7** Turn over and fold a flap down at the top.

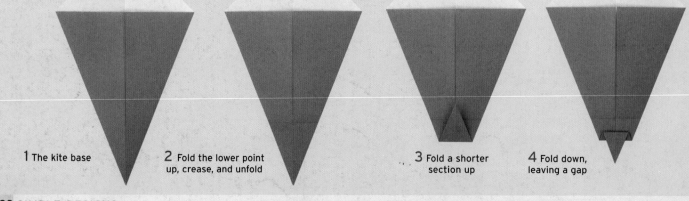

→ **WATCH THE MODEL FOLD UP...**

1 The kite base

2 Fold the lower point up, crease, and unfold

3 Fold a shorter section up

4 Fold down, leaving a gap

▶ **8** Valley fold (see page 14) the paper in half on the vertical center crease.

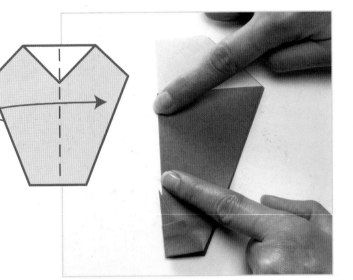

◀ **9** Hold the head and body at the circled points (the penguin is upside-down at this stage), then ease the head outward, flattening the paper when in position.

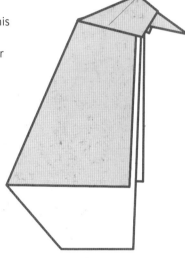

▲ **10** Turn the finished penguin right side up.

5 & 6 Refold the step 2 crease

7 Turn over and fold the top point down

8 Fold in half

9 Ease out the head

10 Rotate to a standing position

Sailboat

This is another delightfully simple traditional design, capturing the subject perfectly with a minimum number of folds. Experiment with the position and angle of the creases and see whether it produces what you consider a better result. At what point does it not look like a sailboat? Many more complex designs rely on the folder's "eye" to position a crease to the best effect, so this is a good model to practice with. For fun, you could sink (see page 25) the base of the model at step 4 instead of folding it behind.

MAKING THE BOAT

▷ **1** Start with a square, colored side up. Fold in half diagonally from left to right.

▷ **2** Fold the lower right (raw) edges over, then unfold.

→ WATCH THE MODEL FOLD UP...

1 Fold diagonally

3 Open out the paper and form an outside reverse fold (see page 20) on the creases.

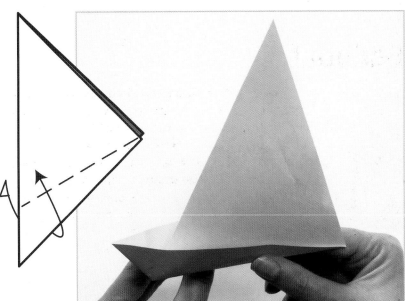

4 Mountain fold (see page 15) part of the lower point behind, on a crease parallel to the raw colored edge. You will probably find it easier to turn the paper over and do the crease as a valley fold, then turn the paper back over afterward.

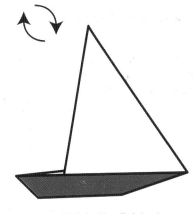

5 Rotate the finished boat clockwise slightly.

2 Crease the lower edge

3 Outside reverse fold

4 Fold back the lower point

5 Rotate so the base is horizontal

Fortune-teller

Instructions for making this traditional design were published more than 150 years ago and the design itself may well be even older. In the West, the model is called "fortune-teller" because you can write messages under the flaps and invite people to choose a number to reflect their personality. In the East, it is known as "saltcellar" and the pockets were used to hold spices.

MAKING THE FORTUNE-TELLER

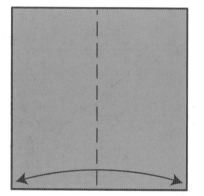

▲ **1** Start with a square, colored side up. Fold in half from side to side, crease, then unfold.

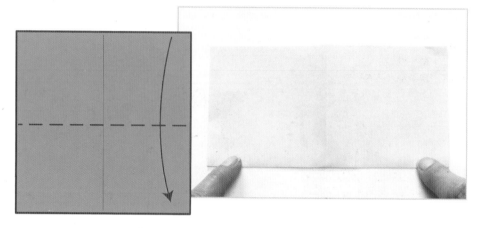

▲ **2** Fold in half from top to bottom. This is easier to do with the fold toward you, but remember to rotate the paper back to the original position afterward.

→ **WATCH THE MODEL FOLD UP...**

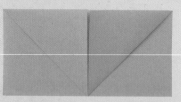

1 Crease in half vertically

2 Fold top to bottom

3 Fold up the two front corners

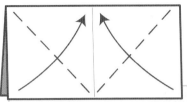

3 Fold each lower corner up to meet the center of the upper folded edge.

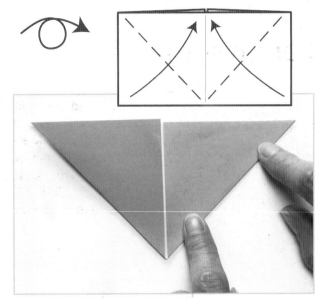

▲ **4** Turn the paper over and repeat step 3 on the other side.

▼ **5** Keeping the four corners folded inward, unfold the upper layer.

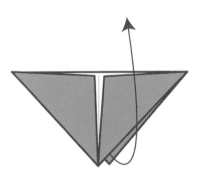

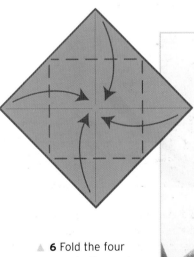

▲ **6** Fold the four corners to the center.

4 Repeat on the other side (photos now enlarged for clarity)

5 Keeping corners folded, open out

6 Fold the new corners to the center

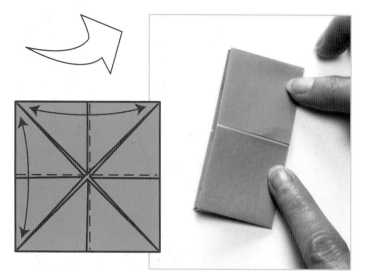

▲ **7** Fold in half from side to side and top to bottom, then unfold. (The diagrams now show an enlarged view of the model.)

▲ **8** Turn the paper over and crease both diagonals.

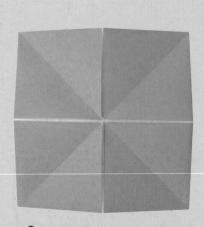

▲ **9** Fold the upper half of the paper behind.

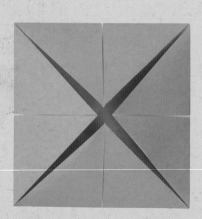

7 Crease in half both ways (photos enlarged again for clarity)

8 Turn over and crease diagonally

9 Fold back the upper half

10 Hold the circled areas and bring your hands together, so the paper forms into the shape of a preliminary base (see page 28).

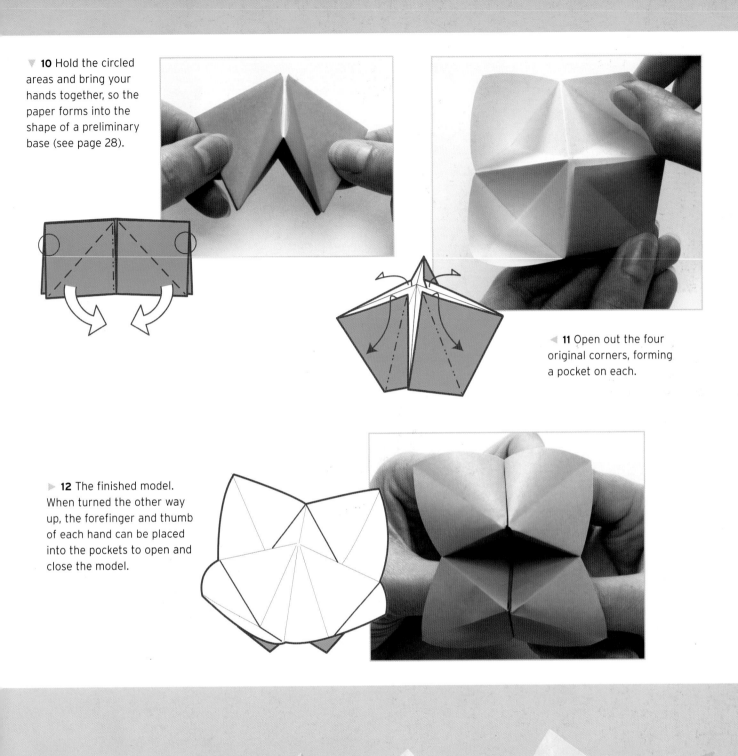

◀ **11** Open out the four original corners, forming a pocket on each.

▶ **12** The finished model. When turned the other way up, the forefinger and thumb of each hand can be placed into the pockets to open and close the model.

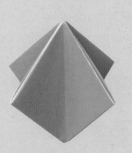

10 Push in the sides

11 Open out the pockets

12 The finished model

Basketball hoop

This is a design that falls in the category of "playground fold"—it is popular among schoolchildren, but nobody knows who came up with the idea in the first place. It requires a rectangular piece of paper rather than a square; a sheet of letter-size (A4) printer paper would be ideal. The sequence starts with the formation of a waterbomb base at the top of the paper. To form the basketball, take a sheet of scrap paper and crumple it into a tight ball!

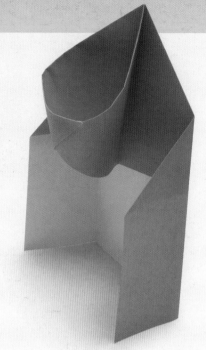

WATERBOMB BASE REMINDER

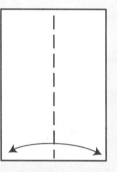

1 Start with a rectangle, white side up. Fold in half from side to side, crease, then unfold.

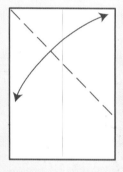

2 Fold the upper short edge to the vertical left edge, crease, then unfold.

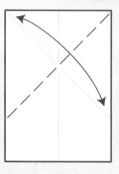

3 Repeat step 2 with the upper short edge to the vertical right edge.

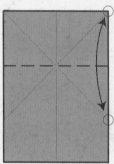

4 Turn the paper over and make a valley fold (see page 14) that passes through the intersection of the creases. The circled points line up. Crease, then unfold.

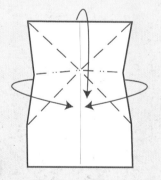

5 Turn the paper back over and collapse it using existing creases.

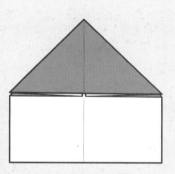

6 The completed waterbomb base formed at one end of the rectangle of paper (see page 30).

MAKING THE HOOP

1 Start with a waterbomb base at the top of the paper (see opposite).

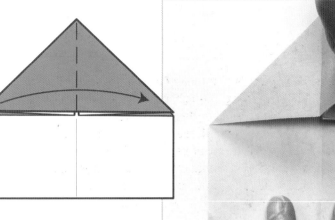

▲ **2** Fold the upper left flap across to the right.

▼ **3** Fold the left vertical edge to the center, crease, then unfold.

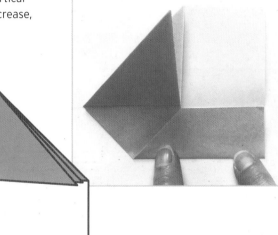

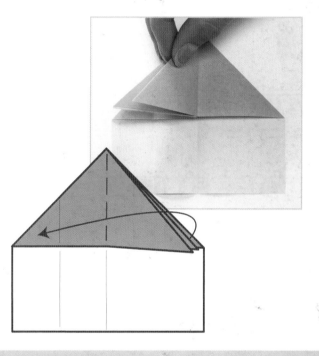

▷ **4** Swing two of the upper flaps from the right to the left.

→ **WATCH THE MODEL FOLD UP...**

1 The waterbomb base

2 Fold the left flap to the right

3 Crease the left edge

4 Swing two flaps from right to left

5 Fold the right vertical edge to the center, crease, then unfold.

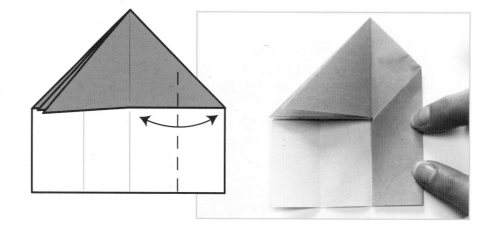

6 Fold a single upper flap from left to right, so there are two flaps on either side.

7 Curl the upper left flap around toward you.

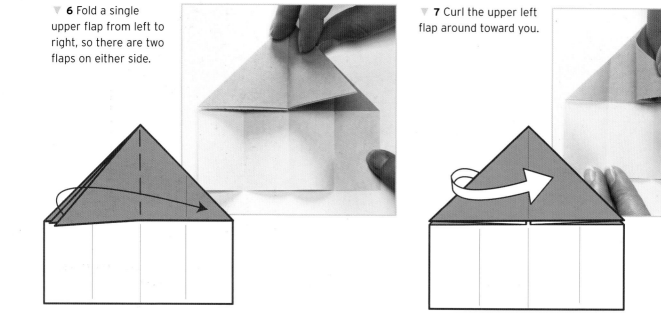

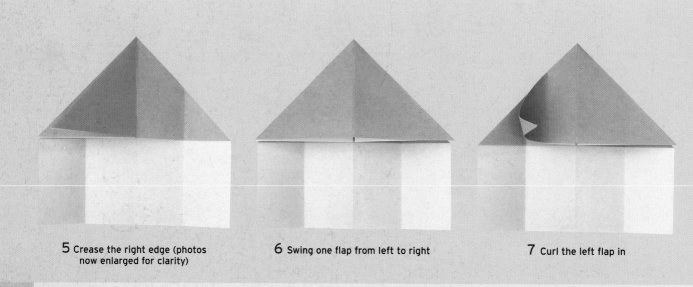

5 Crease the right edge (photos now enlarged for clarity)

6 Swing one flap from left to right

7 Curl the left flap in

8 Repeat with the upper right flap, tucking it into the layers of the other flap so that a hole is left in the middle.

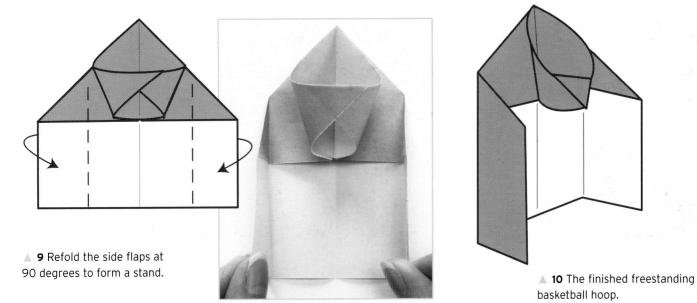

9 Refold the side flaps at 90 degrees to form a stand.

10 The finished freestanding basketball hoop.

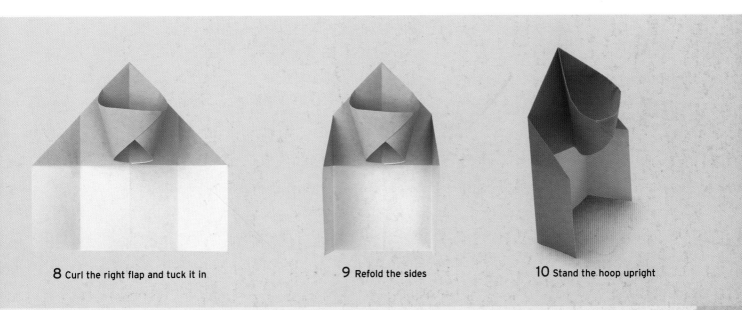

8 Curl the right flap and tuck it in

9 Refold the sides

10 Stand the hoop upright

Banger

This traditional design is fun for both young and old. It works from rectangles of almost any shape, but try to choose paper that is reasonably strong or it will split after a few bangs. The larger the initial sheet, the louder the bang. One fun game is for two people to fold a banger each, then unfold the sheets and lay them on the floor. After a 1, 2, 3 countdown, each person refolds their banger as quickly as possible and tries to "shoot" their opponent first.

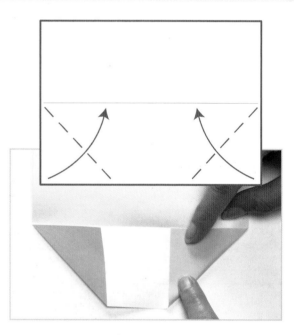

MAKING THE BANGER

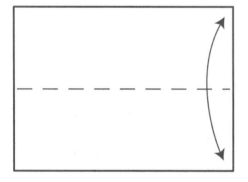

◀ **1** Start with a rectangle of paper, such as a letter-size (A4) sheet of printer paper, white side up. Fold the long edges together, crease firmly, then unfold.

▶ **2** Fold the lower half of each short edge to meet the horizontal crease.

→ **WATCH THE MODEL FOLD UP...**

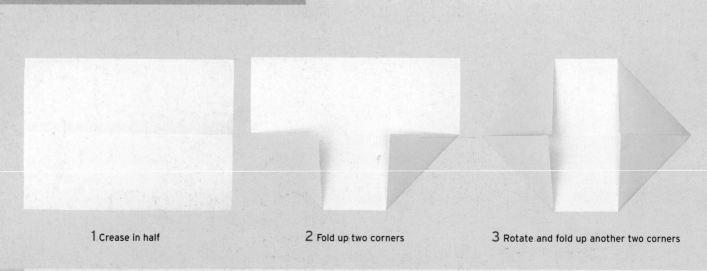

1 Crease in half   **2** Fold up two corners   **3** Rotate and fold up another two corners

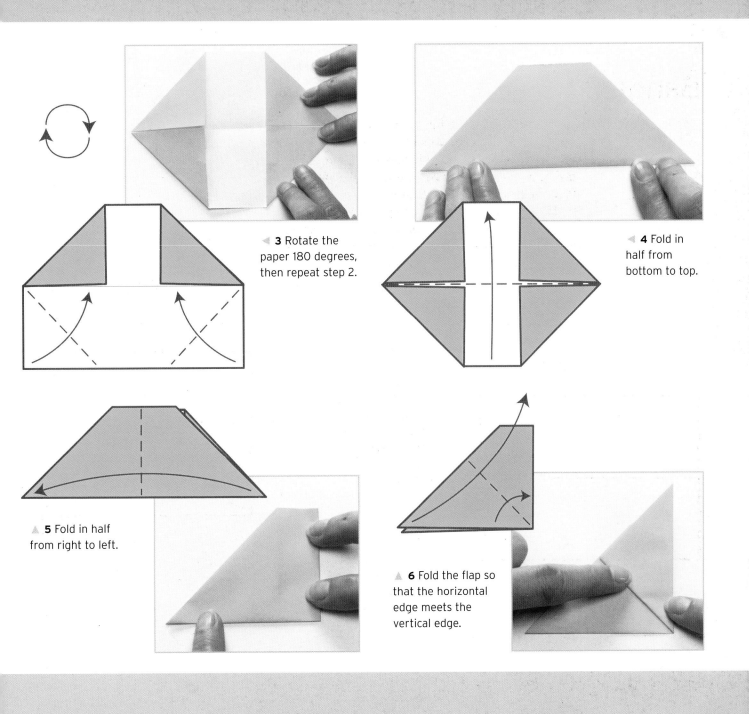

3 Rotate the paper 180 degrees, then repeat step 2.

4 Fold in half from bottom to top.

5 Fold in half from right to left.

6 Fold the flap so that the horizontal edge meets the vertical edge.

4 Fold in half one way (photos now enlarged for clarity)

5 Fold in half the other way

6 Fold the flap up

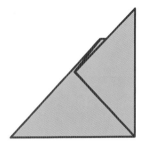

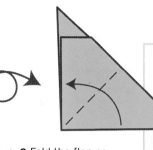

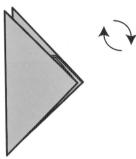

△ **7** This is the result. Turn the paper over.

△ **8** Fold the flap so that the horizontal edge meets the vertical edge.

△ **9** This is the result. Turn the paper about 90 degrees clockwise.

▶ **10** Hold by the circled flaps, flick rapidly up and then downward, and bang. You need to hold it exactly as shown or it will not work—try to see it as an arrowhead that must be facing downward.

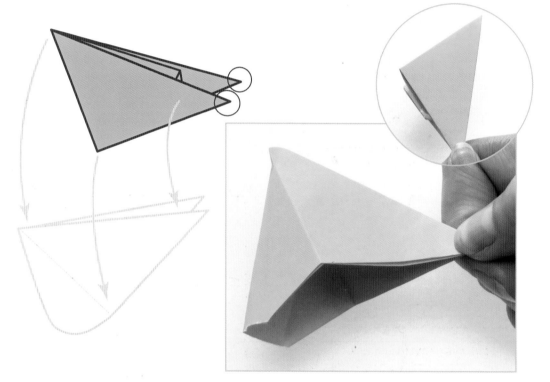

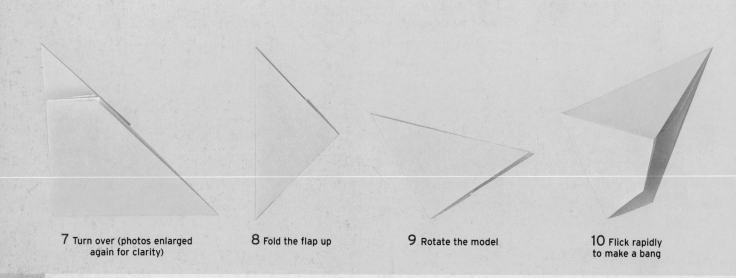

7 Turn over (photos enlarged again for clarity)

8 Fold the flap up

9 Rotate the model

10 Flick rapidly to make a bang

Finger puppet

This is a variation of a design by the late Rene Lucio of Germany. His design started from a rectangle, but I adapted it to work from a square and made other small changes. This type of adaptation is at the heart of creative origami, building on the work of others, but it is important to acknowledge where the idea came from and give credit where it is due. This is a wonderful, simple puppet and you can draw a pair of eyes to add the final touches if you wish. Philip Blencoe from the UK coined the term "birogami" for designs that are enhanced with drawn features.

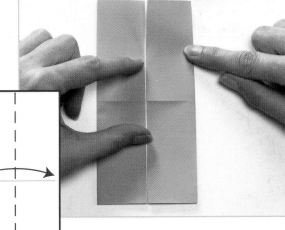

MAKING THE PUPPET

1 Start with a square, white side up. Fold in half from side to side and top to bottom, crease, then unfold.

2 Fold left and right edges to the vertical center crease. Crease and unfold.

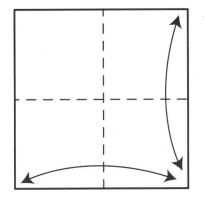

3 Fold the lower edge to the center.

→ WATCH THE MODEL FOLD UP...

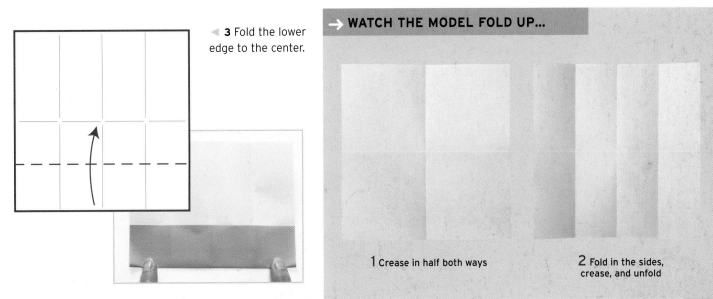

1 Crease in half both ways

2 Fold in the sides, crease, and unfold

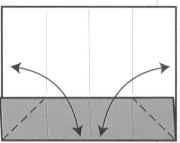

▲ **4** Add diagonal valley creases (see page 14), though all layers, in the lower corners.

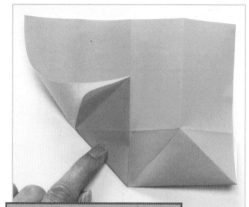

▶ **5** Turn the paper over and add two more diagonal creases.

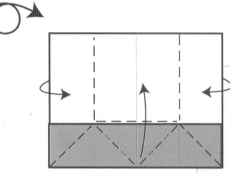

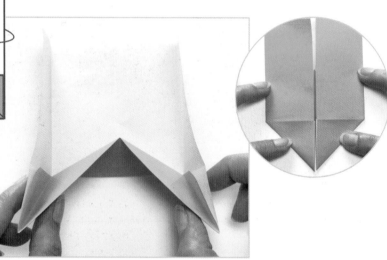

▲ **6** Turn the paper over again and use the creases to collapse the paper. No new creases are needed.

3 Fold up the lower edge

4 Crease the corners

5 Crease diagonally again

6 Turn over and collapse the paper (photos now enlarged for clarity)

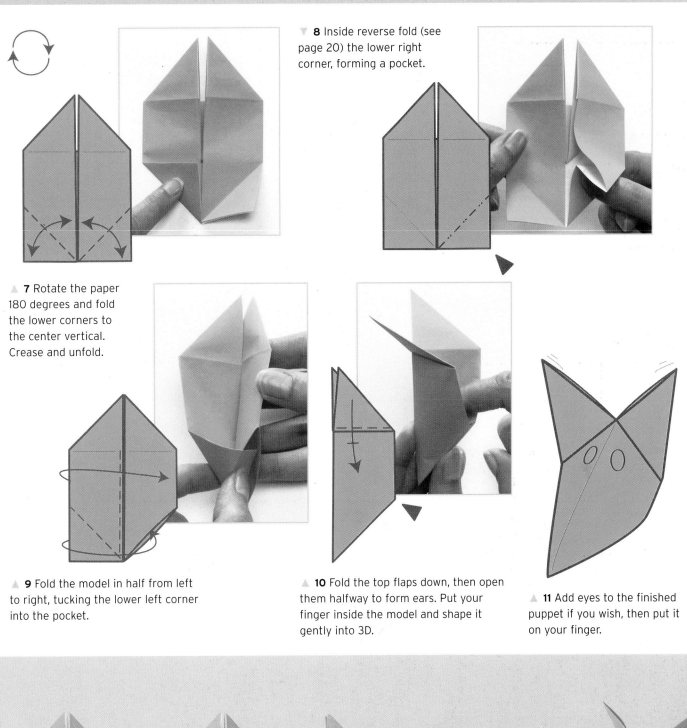

8 Inside reverse fold (see page 20) the lower right corner, forming a pocket.

7 Rotate the paper 180 degrees and fold the lower corners to the center vertical. Crease and unfold.

9 Fold the model in half from left to right, tucking the lower left corner into the pocket.

10 Fold the top flaps down, then open them halfway to form ears. Put your finger inside the model and shape it gently into 3D.

11 Add eyes to the finished puppet if you wish, then put it on your finger.

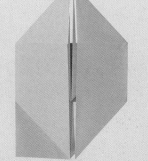

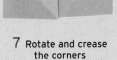

7 Rotate and crease the corners

8 Inside reverse fold

9 Fold in half and tuck in the bottom corner

10 Fold the ears and form the head into 3D

11 The finished puppet

Jaws 1

This is my own design and is an attempt to create origami that reflects subjects as they might be seen in real life. The first sheet of paper forms a shark emerging from the water, with the tip of the tail fin created from a second, smaller sheet. Although I have tried extending the initial design, adding more features (including a victim held in the mouth) and consequent complexity, there comes a point where you lose the simplicity of the form. A slightly more advanced version of this design (with a lower jaw) is on page 94.

MAKING THE BODY

▲ **1** Start with a square, white side up. Fold and unfold on the vertical diagonal.

◀ **2** Fold the top corner to the bottom corner. This is easier to do accurately with the fold toward you, but you will need to rotate the paper afterward.

▽ **3** Fold the lower corner (first layer only) to somewhere near the circled point.

→ **WATCH THE MODEL FOLD UP...**

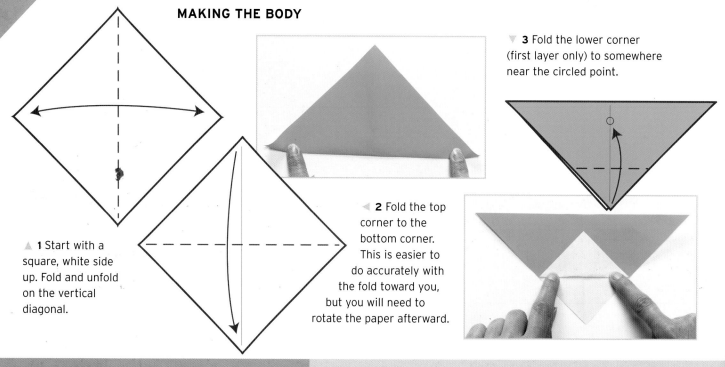

1 Crease diagonally

2 Fold top to bottom

3 Fold up the bottom corner

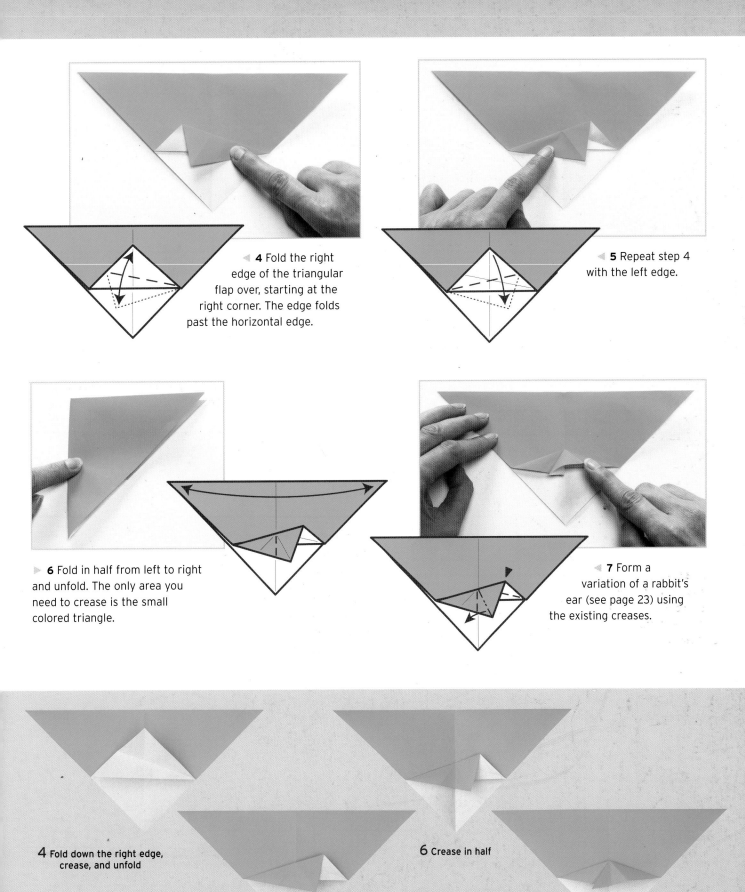

4 Fold the right edge of the triangular flap over, starting at the right corner. The edge folds past the horizontal edge.

5 Repeat step 4 with the left edge.

6 Fold in half from left to right and unfold. The only area you need to crease is the small colored triangle.

7 Form a variation of a rabbit's ear (see page 23) using the existing creases.

4 Fold down the right edge, crease, and unfold

5 Fold down the left edge

6 Crease in half

7 Form a rabbit's ear

8 Fold the two upper corners to the lower corner. Allow the rabbit's ear to protrude at the center.

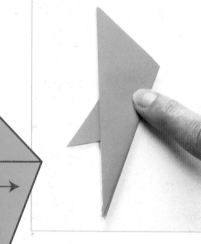

9 Turn the paper over and fold the lower edges to the center. (The diagrams now show an enlarged view of the model.)

10 Fold the model in half from left to right. Let the rabbit's ear pop out to become the fin.

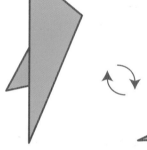

11 The shark's body is complete.

12 Rotate clockwise to the correct position.

8 Fold down the top two corners, letting the rabbit's ear pop out (photos now enlarged for clarity)

9 Turn over and fold the edges in

10 Fold in half

11 & 12 Rotate the finished body

MAKING THE TAIL

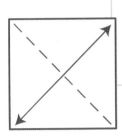

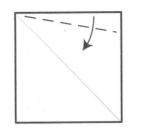

◀ **13** Start with a square, white side up. It should be much smaller than the square for the body. Fold and unfold on one diagonal.

▲ **14** Fold over a narrow flap, starting at the top left corner.

▲ **15** Refold on the diagonal crease.

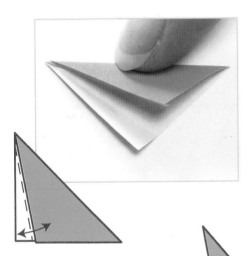

◀ **17** Refold the left edge, tucking it inside the layers.

▲ **16** Fold the left raw edge over the folded edge, crease, and unfold.

◀ **18** Arrange the tail behind the body to complete the shark.

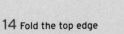

13 Crease the tail diagonally (photos enlarged again for clarity)

14 Fold the top edge

15 Refold diagonally

16 Crease the other edge

17 Tuck in the flap

18 The finished shark

Crown

Another traditional design that is known all over the world, this is a beautifully economical sequence that allows anyone to follow it, including beginners, and produces a wonderful finished object. If you have made a few and are feeling confident, try the variations and then see if you can discover a new one of your own.

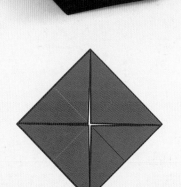

BLINTZ BASE REMINDER

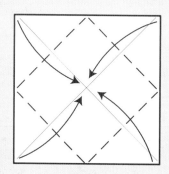

1 Start with a square, white side up. Fold and unfold both diagonals.

2 Fold all four corners to the center.

3 The completed blintz base (see page 27).

MAKING THE CROWN

1 Start with a blintz base (see above), with the folded corners on the reverse side.

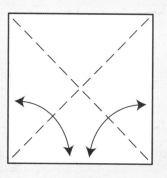

◄ **2** Fold upper and lower edges to the center, allowing the flaps to pop out from underneath.

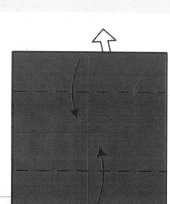

→ WATCH THE MODEL FOLD UP...

1 The blintz base

2 Fold over the edges, letting the flaps pop out

▼ **3** Fold the lower triangular flap upward.

▼ **4** Fold in the lower small colored triangles.

▼ **5** Fold both upper flaps downward.

▼ **6** Fold in the upper small colored triangles.

3 Fold up the bottom flap

4 Fold up the lower triangles

5 Fold down both flaps

6 Fold down the upper triangles

7 Fold a single flap back upward.

8 Carefully open out the pocket at the center, forming the crown into 3D.

9 Pinch the edges to make them sharp.

10 Turn over to reveal the finished crown.

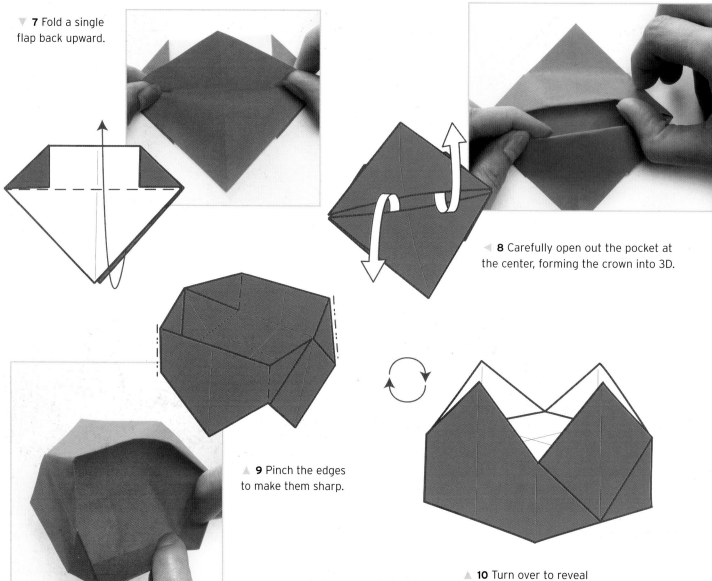

7 Fold up one flap (photos now enlarged for clarity)

8 Open out from the center

9 Pinch the edges

10 Turn over for the finished crown

BOX VARIATION

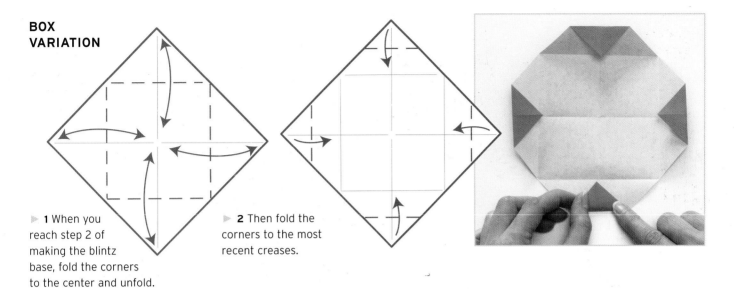

1 When you reach step 2 of making the blintz base, fold the corners to the center and unfold.

2 Then fold the corners to the most recent creases.

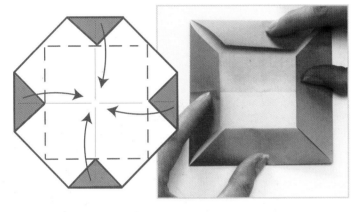

3 Fold over again on the creases indicated.

4 Turn over and continue from step 2 of the main sequence. The result will be a box.

POLYHEDRON VARIATION

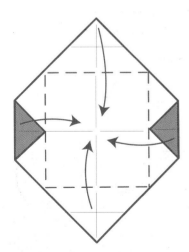

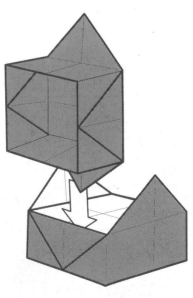

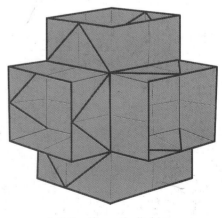

1 Follow to the end of step 2 of the box variation, then unfold two opposite corners. Carry out the instruction above, turn over, then continue from step 2 of the main sequence. This will produce a box with two flaps and two pockets.

2 Make six identical boxes, then slide the flap of one box into the pocket of the next.

3 Continue at all sides to produce an interesting geometric polyhedron.

Star box

This traditional design uses simple techniques to produce a beautiful and unexpected result. The squash move in step 3 seems slightly strange to new folders, but it is a useful technique and the name perfectly describes the move itself. With all similar boxes, it helps to concentrate on accurate creasing in order to achieve a perfectly symmetrical model.

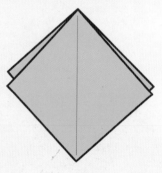

PRELIMINARY BASE REMINDER

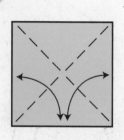 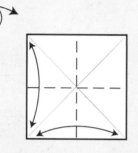 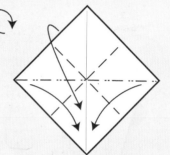

1 Fold both diagonals, crease, and unfold.

2 Turn over and fold in half both ways. Crease and unfold.

3 Rotate 45 degrees, then collapse the paper along the existing creases.

4 The completed preliminary base (see page 28).

MAKING THE BOX

1 Start with a preliminary base (see above).

2 Fold the lower right flap to the vertical center crease.

→ **WATCH THE MODEL FOLD UP...**

1 The preliminary base

2 Fold in one flap

3 Lift and squash the flap (see page 24), aligning the edges and creases carefully.

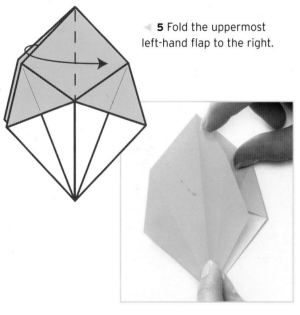

4 This is the result. Repeat steps 2 and 3 with the lower left flap, then repeat on the other side.

5 Fold the uppermost left-hand flap to the right.

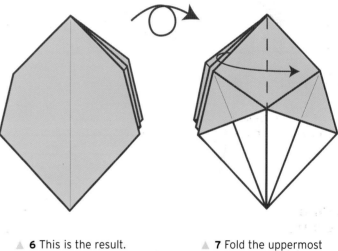

6 This is the result. Turn the paper over.

7 Fold the uppermost left-hand flap to the right.

3 Squash the flap

4 Repeat with the other three flaps

5 Fold a flap across from left to right

6 Turn the paper over

7 Fold another flap across from left to right

8 Fold the lower left edge to the center vertical crease.

9 This is the result. Repeat step 8 with the lower right edge, then repeat on the other side.

10 Rotate the paper 180 degrees. Fold the lower flap upward between the widest points. Crease firmly and unfold.

11 Fold the topmost layer of the upper flap down as far as it will go. Repeat the move on the matching flap on the other side.

8 Fold the lower left edge (photos now enlarged for clarity)

9 Repeat with the other three lower edges

10 Rotate, fold the bottom point up, crease, and unfold

11 Fold the first layer of the top point down

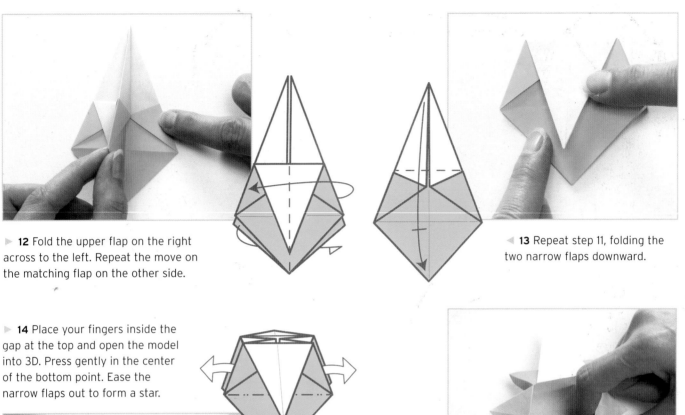

12 Fold the upper flap on the right across to the left. Repeat the move on the matching flap on the other side.

13 Repeat step 11, folding the two narrow flaps downward.

14 Place your fingers inside the gap at the top and open the model into 3D. Press gently in the center of the bottom point. Ease the narrow flaps out to form a star.

15 Sharpen the creases around the base.

12 Fold a flap across from right to left, then repeat on the other side

13 Fold the top point down

14 Open out the model to form a star shape (shown here from above)

15 Sharpen the creases to complete the box

Tulip

This traditional design was discovered relatively recently. Some say it has origins in Thailand, but we cannot be sure. It is certainly unusual, because it employs the same technique as the waterbomb (see page 72) to inflate the model at the end. It is not possible to tuck the flaps deeply into each other during steps 7 and 8, but you can get enough paper in for it to hold in place while you complete the model.

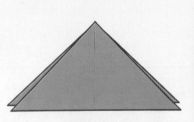

WATERBOMB BASE REMINDER

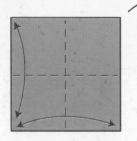

1 Start with a square, colored side up, and crease in half both ways.

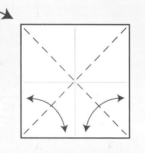

2 Turn the paper over and crease both diagonals.

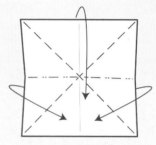

3 Collapse the paper using the creases.

4 The completed waterbomb base (see page 30).

MAKING THE TULIP

1 Start with a waterbomb base (see above).

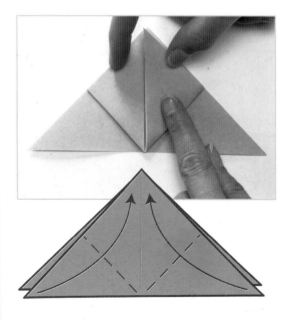

▲ **2** Fold both lower corners up to the top corner.

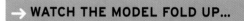

→ **WATCH THE MODEL FOLD UP...**

1 The waterbomb base

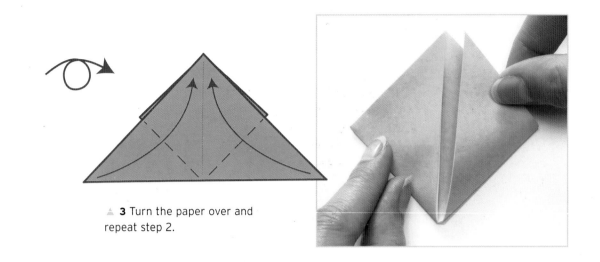

3 Turn the paper over and repeat step 2.

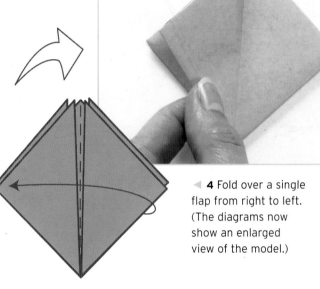

4 Fold over a single flap from right to left. (The diagrams now show an enlarged view of the model.)

5 Turn the paper over and fold over a single flap from right to left. There should now be two flaps on either side.

2 Fold up the two lower corners

3 Turn over and repeat

4 Fold a flap from right to left

5 Turn over and fold another flap from right to left

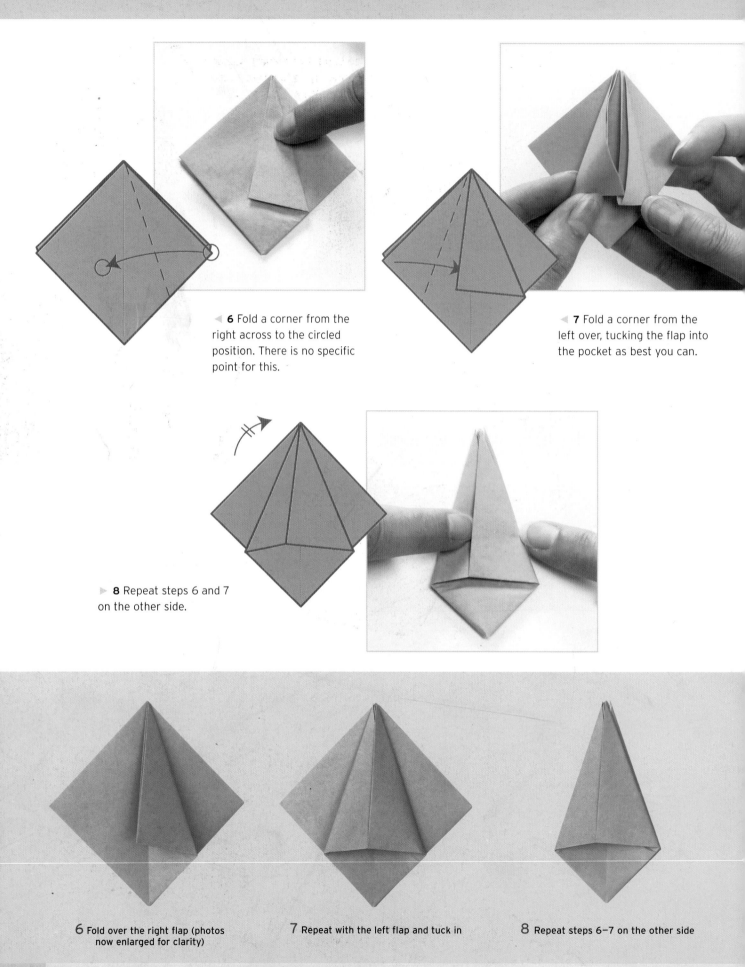

6 Fold a corner from the right across to the circled position. There is no specific point for this.

7 Fold a corner from the left over, tucking the flap into the pocket as best you can.

8 Repeat steps 6 and 7 on the other side.

6 Fold over the right flap (photos now enlarged for clarity)

7 Repeat with the left flap and tuck in

8 Repeat steps 6–7 on the other side

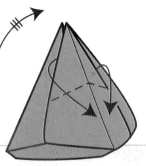

10 Carefully peel back one of the outer layers to form a petal. Repeat on the three other flaps.

9 Open the model slightly and blow into the hole at the base, encouraging the paper into 3D.

11 The finished tulip.

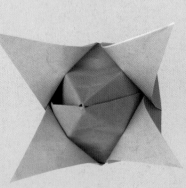

9 Open out and inflate

10 Peel back the petals one at a time (shown here from above)

11 The finished tulip

Waterbomb

This design is more than 100 years old and was used by young children in the East to store captured flies, which would buzz around inside. It also has a richly deserved notoriety in schools all around the world, where it is filled with water and thrown at an enemy. Without encouraging this activity, it is best to fill and then hold the model for a minute or two to allow the paper to soak through so that it will explode more effectively.

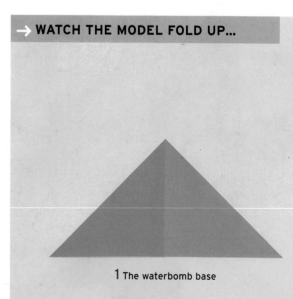

WATERBOMB BASE REMINDER

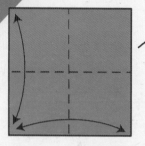
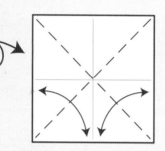
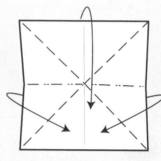
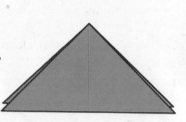

1 Start with a square, colored side up, crease in half both ways, then unfold.

2 Turn the paper over and crease both diagonals.

3 Collapse the paper using the creases.

4 The completed waterbomb base (see page 30).

MAKING THE WATERBOMB

1 Start with a waterbomb base (see above).

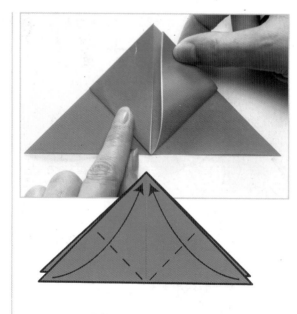

▲ **2** Fold both lower corners up to the top corner.

→ **WATCH THE MODEL FOLD UP...**

1 The waterbomb base

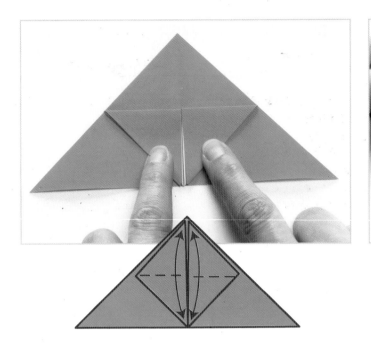

3 Fold the two loose corners at the top to the bottom center point, crease, and unfold.

4 Fold the left and right corners to meet at the center.

5 One side is complete. Repeat steps 2–4 on the other side.

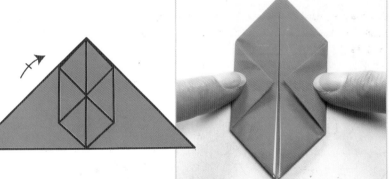

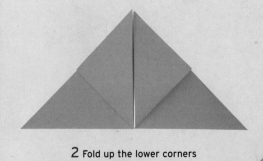

2 Fold up the lower corners

3 Fold down the top corners, crease, then unfold

4 Fold the small triangles inward

5 Repeat steps 2–4 on the other side

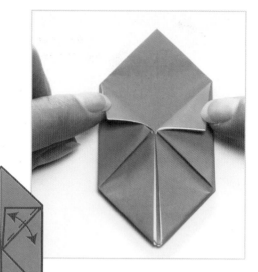

◄ **6** Fold the two loose corners at the top to the center. (The diagrams now show an enlarged view of the model.)

◄ **7** Fold the small triangular flaps over the folded edge, crease, and unfold.

► **8** Carefully tuck the same flaps into matching pockets.

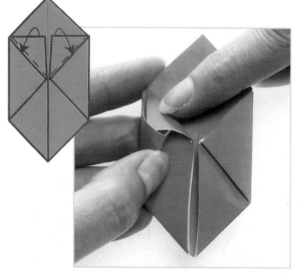

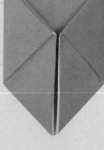

6 Fold down the loose top corners (photos now enlarged for clarity)

7 Crease the small triangular flaps outward

8 Tuck them in

9 Repeat steps 6–8 on the other side

◄ **9** Repeat steps 6–8 on the other side.

▶ **10** Fold the top and bottom corners to the center, crease firmly, and unfold.

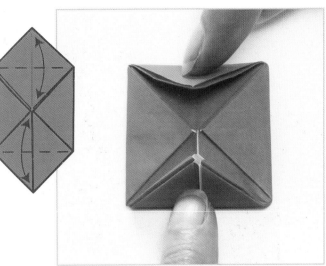

◄ **11** Open the layers slightly and encourage the paper to open as you blow sharply into the hole at the bottom point of the paper.

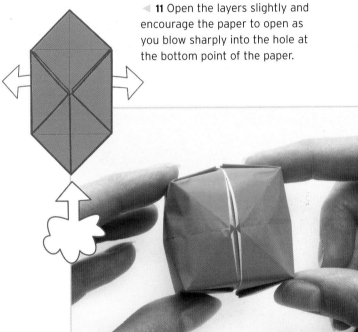

▼ **12** Sharpen the edges by pinching them to form a cube. Fill with water just before use.

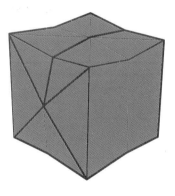

10 Fold the top and bottom corners inward, crease, and unfold

11 Open out and inflate (shown here from below)

12 Use the hole to fill the finished waterbomb with water

Butterfly

A design that probably started with work by the Japanese master Akira Yoshizawa, this model uses the folding sequence of the multiform base to form the wings. You can make different-shaped lower wings by altering the folds made in step 4. Try to choose paper that looks like a real butterfly and see if you can fold it smaller and smaller until it is the same size as a real butterfly.

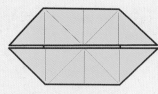

MULTIFORM BASE REMINDER

1 Start with a square, white side up. Fold in half from side to side and top to bottom, crease, then unfold.

2 Crease both diagonals.

3 Turn the paper over and fold each corner to the center. Crease and unfold. Turn the paper back over.

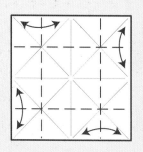

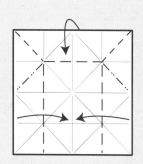

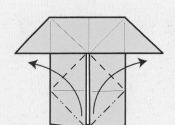

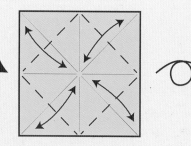

4 Fold each edge to the center. Crease and unfold.

5 Use the creases indicated to collapse the paper—no new creases are needed.

6 Collapse the lower section to match the top.

7 The completed multiform base (see page 31).

MAKING THE BUTTERFLY

1 Start with a multiform base (see opposite).

▼ **2** Mountain fold (see page 15) in half.

▼ **3** Swing the two flaps downward.

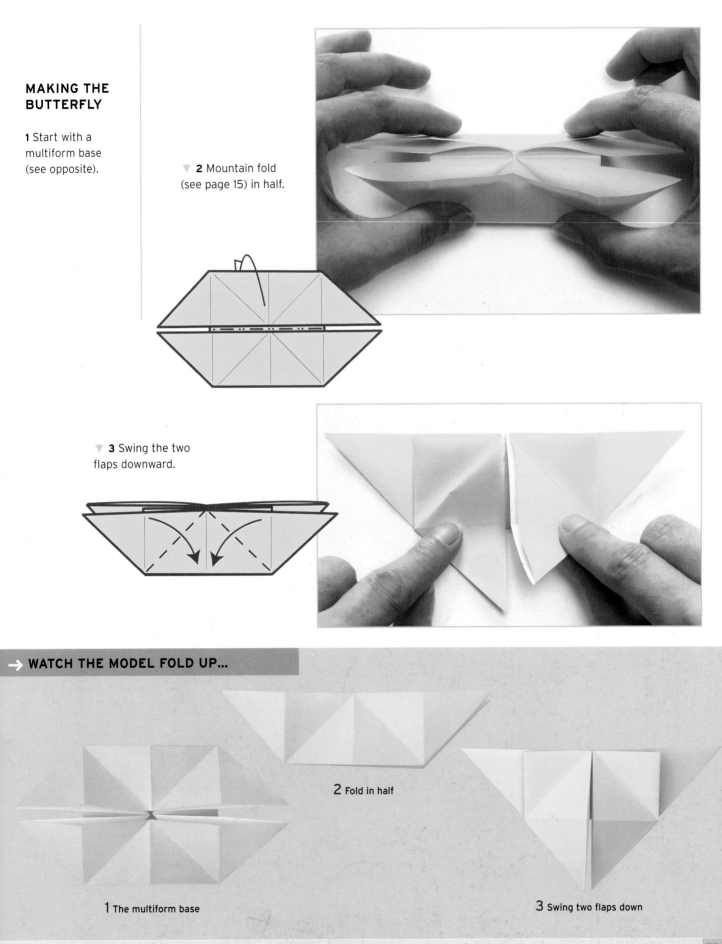

→ WATCH THE MODEL FOLD UP...

2 Fold in half

1 The multiform base

3 Swing two flaps down

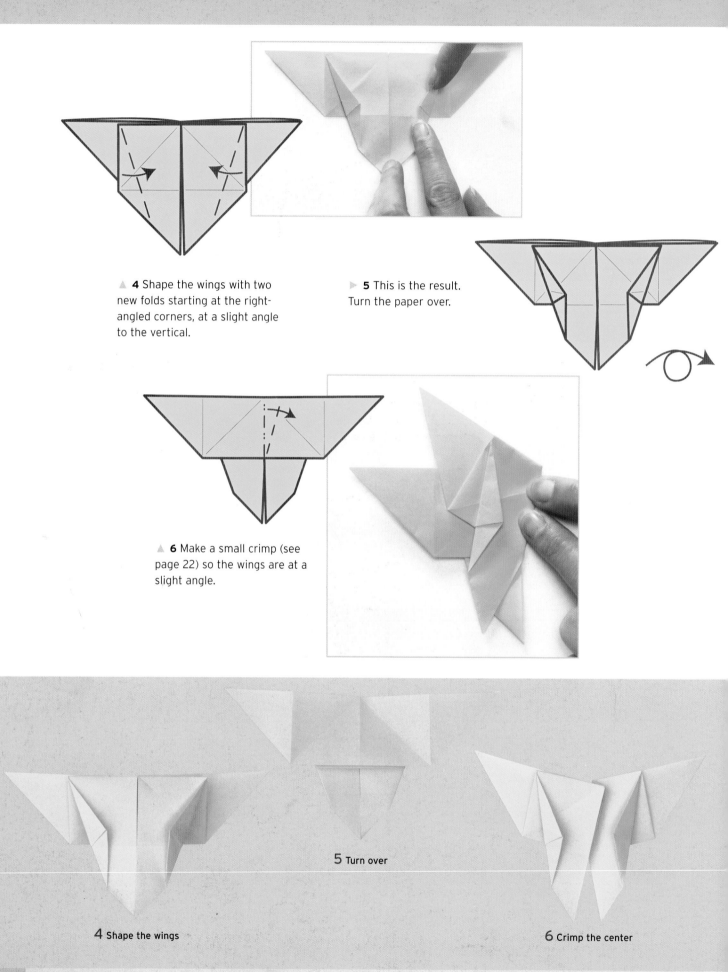

▲ **4** Shape the wings with two new folds starting at the right-angled corners, at a slight angle to the vertical.

▶ **5** This is the result. Turn the paper over.

▲ **6** Make a small crimp (see page 22) so the wings are at a slight angle.

4 Shape the wings

5 Turn over

6 Crimp the center

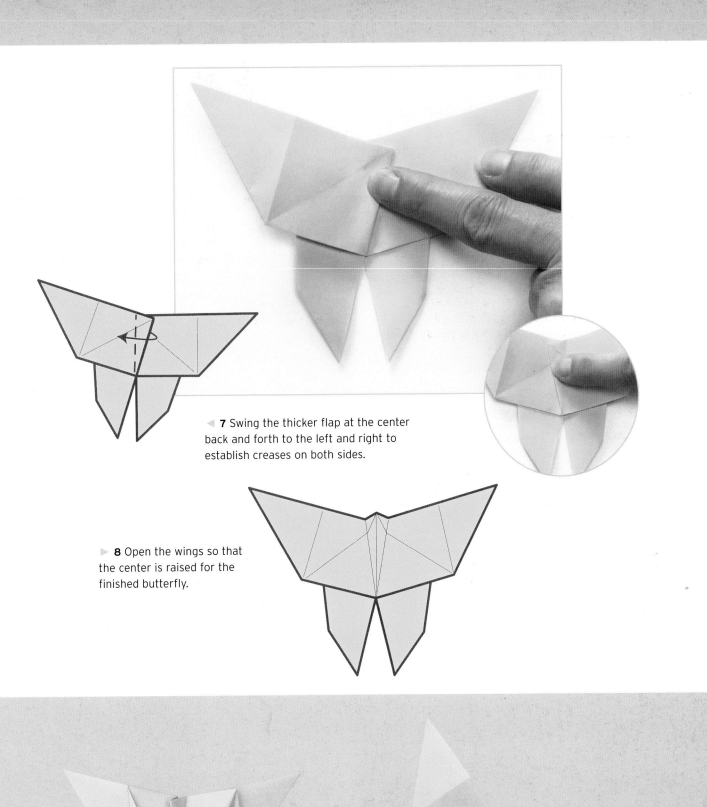

7 Swing the thicker flap at the center back and forth to the left and right to establish creases on both sides.

8 Open the wings so that the center is raised for the finished butterfly.

7 Swing the crimp back and forth to crease it on both sides

8 Open the wings and raise the center to complete the butterfly

Sanbow (Box with legs)

This is a traditional design that has been known for many years. It begins with a blintz base that is then folded and collapsed into a preliminary base and uses a logical sequence to produce a box with four legs. The move in step 5 is unexpected and interesting, as the surplus paper built up by the blintz is partially released.

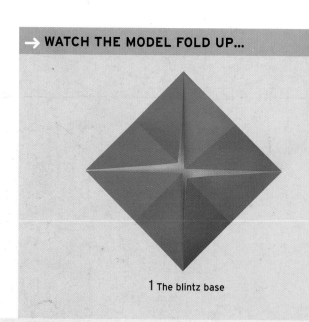

BLINTZ BASE REMINDER

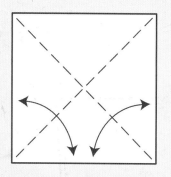

1 Start with a square, white side up. Fold and unfold both diagonals. These diagonal creases are used for collapsing the blintz base into a preliminary base in step 3 of the main sequence.

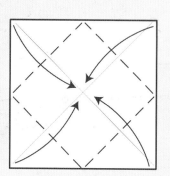

2 Fold all four corners into the center.

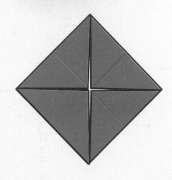

3 The completed blintz base (see page 27).

MAKING THE SANBOW

1 Start with a blintz base (see above).

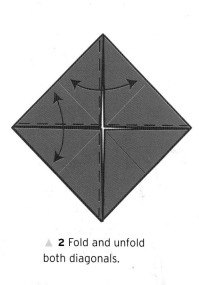

▲ **2** Fold and unfold both diagonals.

→ **WATCH THE MODEL FOLD UP...**

1 The blintz base

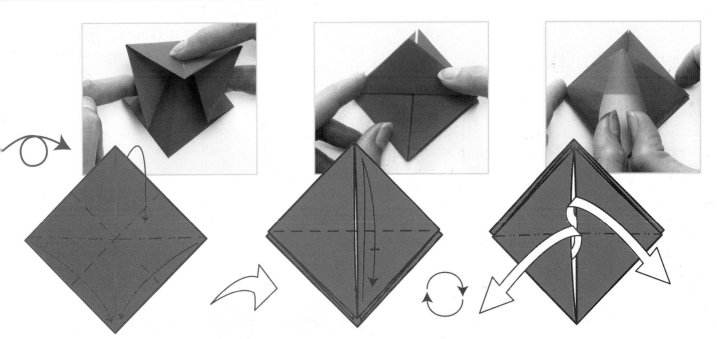

3 Turn the paper over and collapse the paper into a preliminary base (see page 28).

4 Fold the lower corner (uppermost layer only) to the top, crease, and unfold. Repeat on the other side. (The diagrams now show an enlarged view of the model.)

5 Rotate the paper 180 degrees. Open out the raw edges and fold this flap of paper down flat.

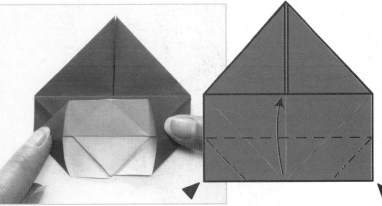

6 Fold the lower raw edge to the folded edge at the center. Put a finger inside the pockets on the left and right to squash (see page 24) the corners neatly.

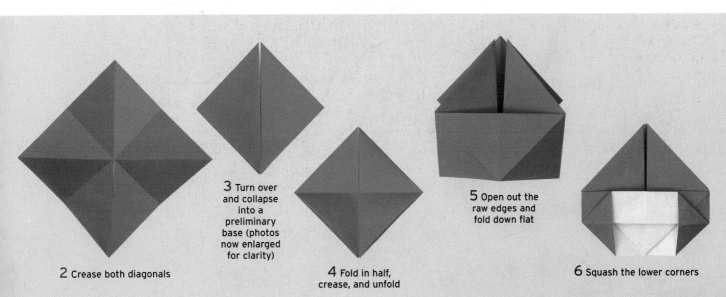

2 Crease both diagonals

3 Turn over and collapse into a preliminary base (photos now enlarged for clarity)

4 Fold in half, crease, and unfold

5 Open out the raw edges and fold down flat

6 Squash the lower corners

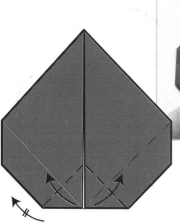

7 This is the result. Repeat steps 5 and 6 on the other side.

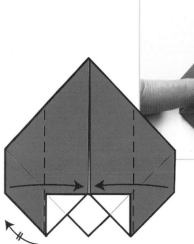

8 Fold the first layer on the left over to the right. Repeat on the other side.

9 Fold two small triangular flaps over at the base of the paper. Repeat on the other side.

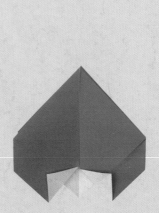

10 Fold left and right sides in to meet at the center. Repeat on the other side.

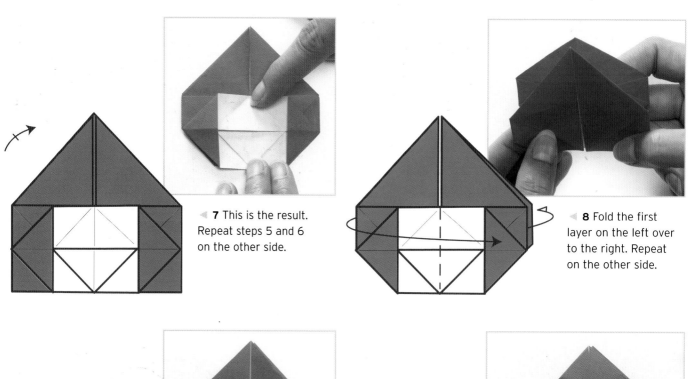

7 Repeat steps 5–6 on the other side

8 Fold one layer from left to right

9 Fold up the triangular base flaps

10 Fold in the sides (photos enlarged again for clarity)

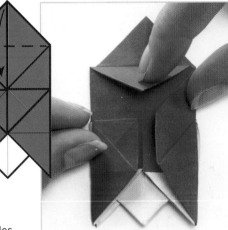
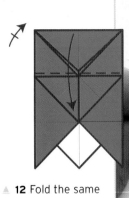

11 Fold the top point down to the center on both sides.

12 Fold the same flap over again on both sides.

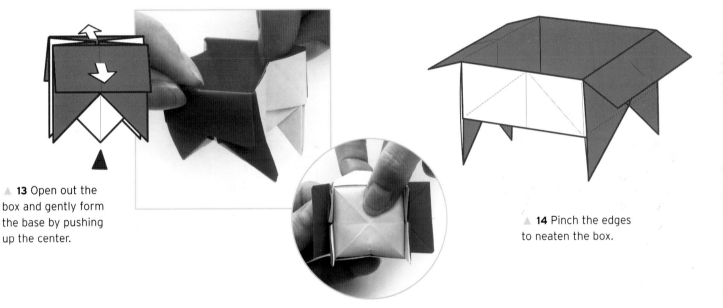

13 Open out the box and gently form the base by pushing up the center.

14 Pinch the edges to neaten the box.

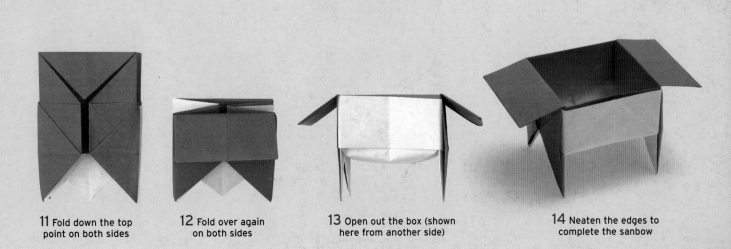

11 Fold down the top point on both sides

12 Fold over again on both sides

13 Open out the box (shown here from another side)

14 Neaten the edges to complete the sanbow

Ninja star

This traditional model is an ingenious design—it uses two units that are almost identical, but are in fact mirror images of one another. You cannot make it by using two identical units. As always, you should fold carefully and neatly if you want the finished result to hold together well and look impressive. Ninja stars make great little gifts for people or you could hang them on a Christmas tree.

MAKING UNIT 1

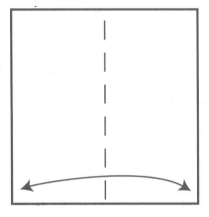

▲ **1** Start with a square, white side up. Fold and unfold from side to side.

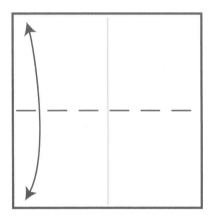

▲ **2** Fold and unfold from top to bottom.

→ WATCH THE MODEL FOLD UP...

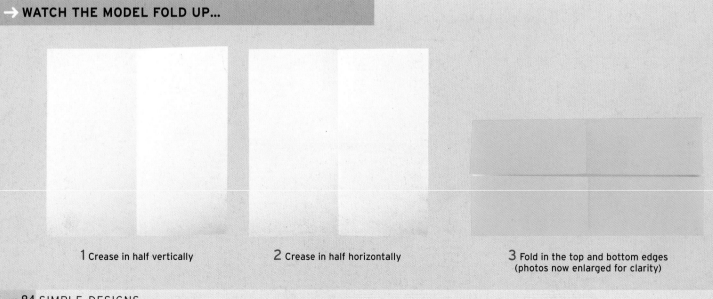

1 Crease in half vertically

2 Crease in half horizontally

3 Fold in the top and bottom edges (photos now enlarged for clarity)

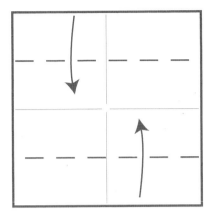

▲ **3** Fold upper and lower edges to the center crease.

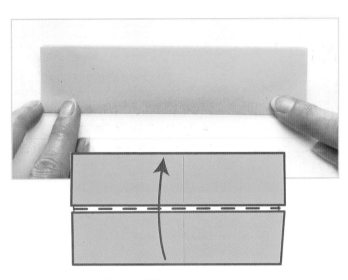

▲ **4** Fold in half from bottom to top.

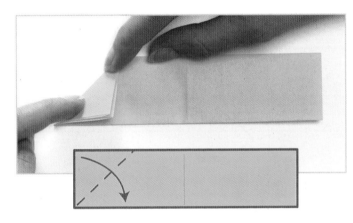

▲ **5** Fold the left-hand short edge down to meet the lower edge.

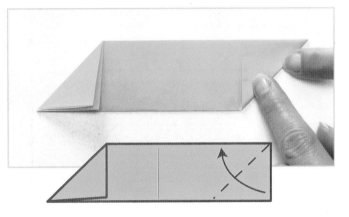

▲ **6** Fold the right-hand short edge up to meet the upper edge.

4 Crease in half

5 Fold down the left corner

6 Fold up the right corner

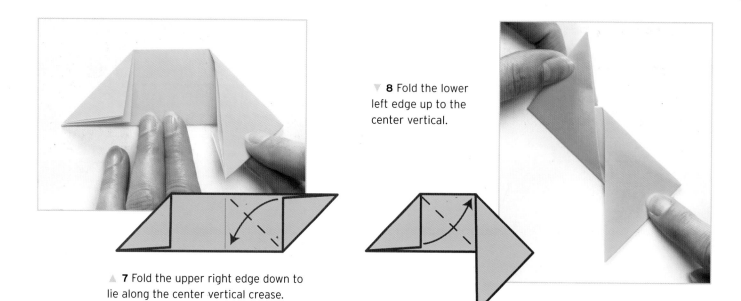

8 Fold the lower left edge up to the center vertical.

7 Fold the upper right edge down to lie along the center vertical crease.

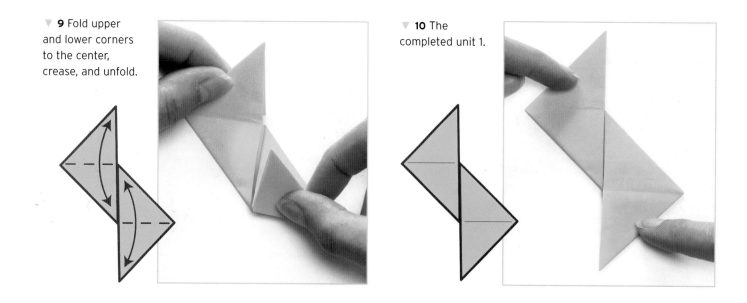

9 Fold upper and lower corners to the center, crease, and unfold.

10 The completed unit 1.

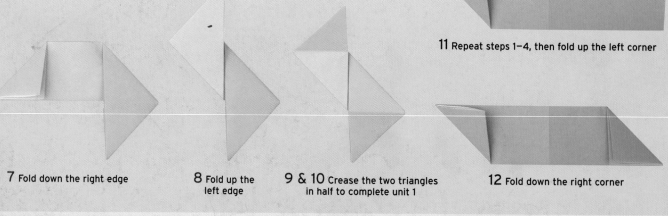

7 Fold down the right edge

8 Fold up the left edge

9 & 10 Crease the two triangles in half to complete unit 1

11 Repeat steps 1–4, then fold up the left corner

12 Fold down the right corner

MAKING UNIT 2

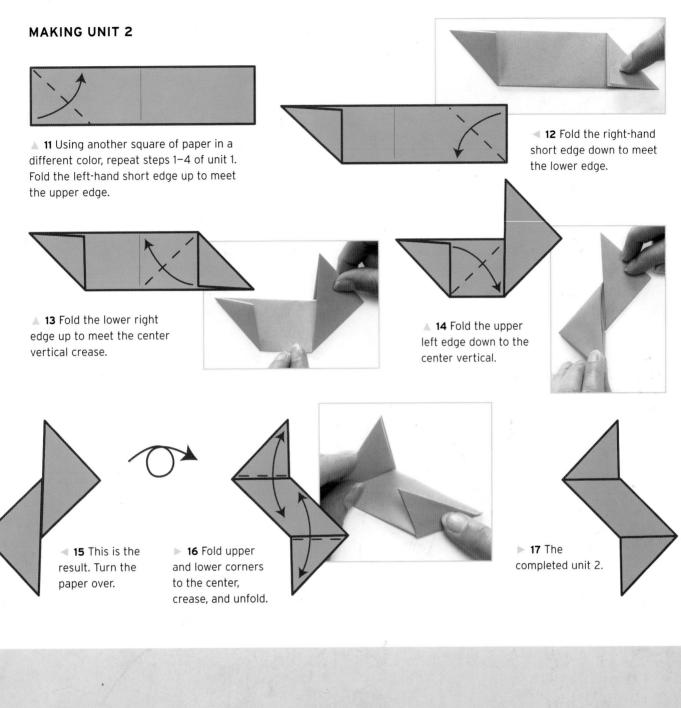

△ **11** Using another square of paper in a different color, repeat steps 1–4 of unit 1. Fold the left-hand short edge up to meet the upper edge.

◁ **12** Fold the right-hand short edge down to meet the lower edge.

△ **13** Fold the lower right edge up to meet the center vertical crease.

△ **14** Fold the upper left edge down to the center vertical.

◁ **15** This is the result. Turn the paper over.

▷ **16** Fold upper and lower corners to the center, crease, and unfold.

▷ **17** The completed unit 2.

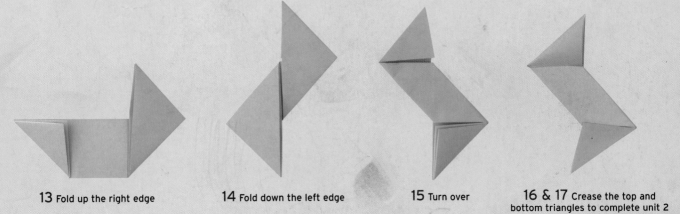

13 Fold up the right edge

14 Fold down the left edge

15 Turn over

16 & 17 Crease the top and bottom triangles to complete unit 2

ASSEMBLING THE STAR

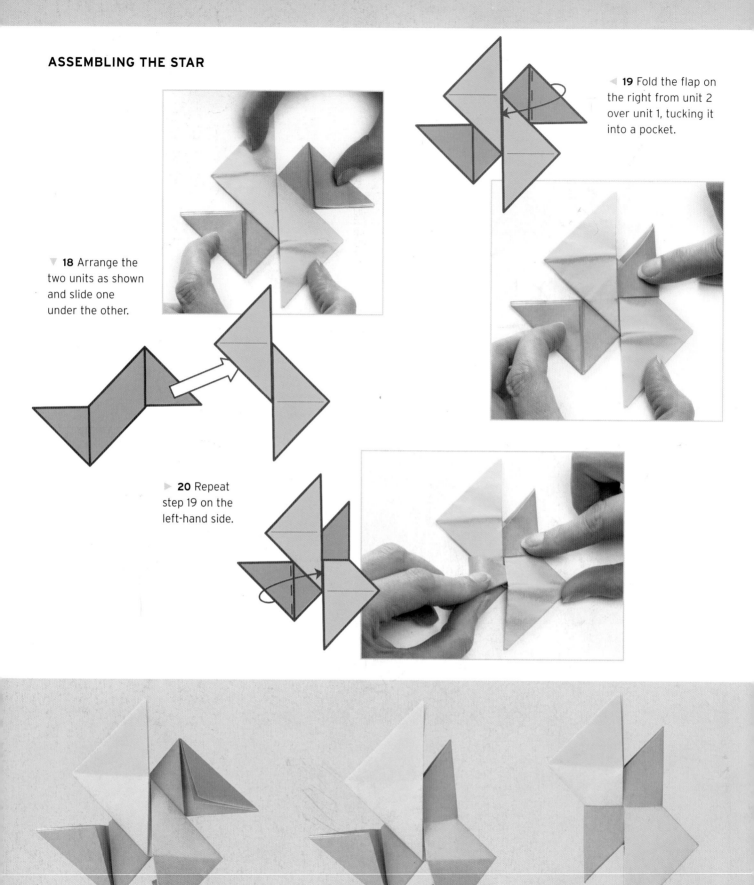

18 Arrange the two units as shown and slide one under the other.

◀ **19** Fold the flap on the right from unit 2 over unit 1, tucking it into a pocket.

▶ **20** Repeat step 19 on the left-hand side.

18 Position one unit on top of the other (photos enlarged again for clarity)

19 Fold and tuck in the first flap

20 Fold and tuck in the second flap

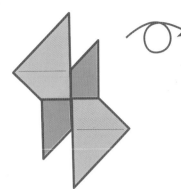

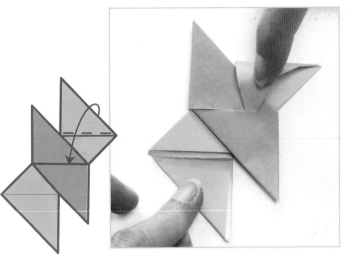

▲ **21** This is the result. Turn the paper over.

▲ **22** Fold the highest corner of unit 1 into a pocket.

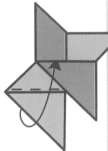

▲ **23** Fold the lowest corner of unit 1 in the same way.

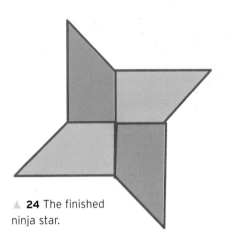

▲ **24** The finished ninja star.

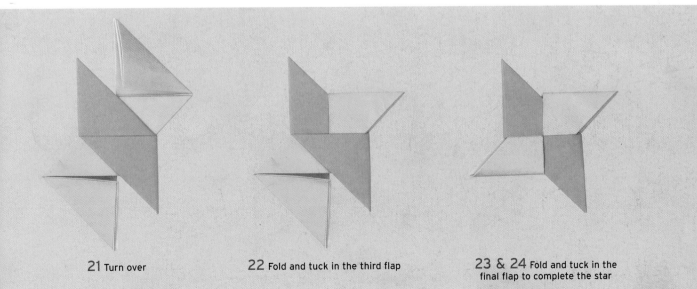

21 Turn over

22 Fold and tuck in the third flap

23 & 24 Fold and tuck in the final flap to complete the star

Contemporary Designs

You will find this selection of designs slightly more challenging
than those in the previous chapter, but nothing here falls into the
"complex" category. If you are a novice folder, use a large piece
of paper for your first attempts. For clarity, all of the diagrams and
instructions refer to origami paper with a color on one side and
white on the other. The models are all designed by contemporary
origami creators. You will see how the subject of the designs varies
widely—origami is only limited by the imagination of the folder.

Gift box

This elegant container, created by Robin Glynn of the UK, and independently by Tomoko Fuse of Japan, is both attractive and functional—your friends will be delighted to receive a gift in it. The assembly stage from step 10 onward will provide a bit of a challenge—you need to handle the paper very gently and may feel you need an extra hand, but it is possible. Until you have the final corner tucked in place, the other corners will try to unfold, but be patient. Try to fold neatly and accurately at all times.

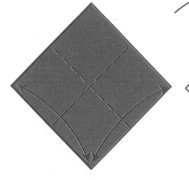 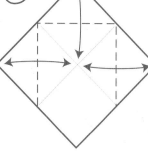 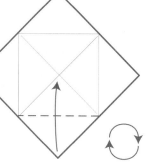 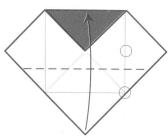

△ **1** Start with a square, colored side up. Fold in half both ways, edge to edge. Crease and unfold.

△ **2** Turn the paper over. Fold three corners to the center, crease, and unfold.

△ **3** Fold the remaining corner to the center. Rotate the paper 180 degrees.

△ **4** Fold the lower corner to the center of the top edge. The circled areas line up.

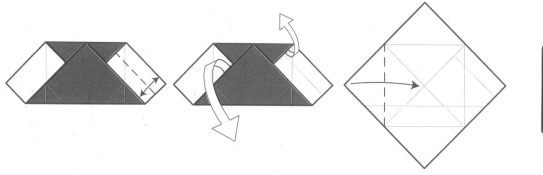 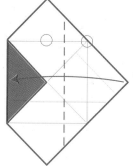

△ **5** Fold the upper right edge to the raw colored edge, crease, and unfold.

△ **6** Unfold the corners to get back to a square.

△ **7** Fold the left corner to the center.

△ **8** Fold the right corner to the center of the left edge. The circled areas line up.

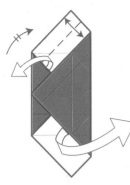

9 Repeat steps 5 and 6, then repeat steps 4–6 on the remaining two corners.

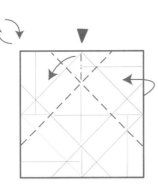

10 Rotate the paper to this position. Raise two sides up at 90 degrees, using the creases indicated.

As you perform step 10, a small flap like a rabbit's ear will form between the two raised sides.

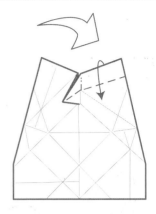

11 Fold the upper right edge over. (The diagrams now show an enlarged view of the model.)

When you fold over the upper right edge in step 11, note that it will not lie flat.

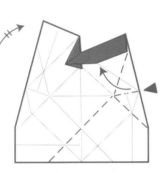

12 Raise the next side on the right in the same way. Repeat twice more, so that all sides of the box are raised.

This is what the box should look like with all four sides raised at the end of step 12.

13 When all four sides are ready, fold one of the layers over halfway.

14 Fold the next corner over, working in a clockwise direction.

15 Continuing clockwise, fold the third corner over.

16 Fold the final corner over, tucking it under the first corner.

17 The finished box.

Jaws 2

This development of the simpler model on page 56 features a lower jaw. This demonstrates how a basic idea can be extended by rearranging the design to provide surplus paper where needed for the extra features. While the final shape is nearly the same, the model itself is smaller, because paper is used in a different, slightly more complicated way. Make the tail following the instructions for the simpler model.

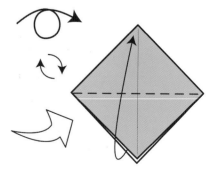

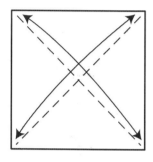

1 Start with a square, white side up. Crease and unfold both diagonals.

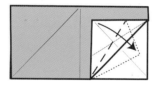

2 Fold the lower edge to the top edge.

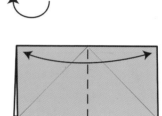

3 Rotate the paper 180 degrees. Fold in half from side to side, crease, and unfold.

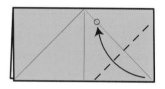

4 Fold the uppermost layer of the lower right corner to the circled point.

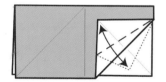

5 Fold the uppermost white corner to the dotted position, crease, and unfold.

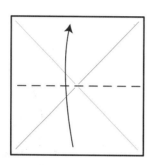

6 Fold the uppermost white corner to the new dotted position, crease, and unfold.

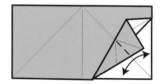

7 Refold the right-hand diagonal, creasing through the extra layers. Unfold.

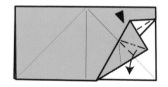

8 Form an offset rabbit's ear in the uppermost flap along the diagonal fold (see next diagram for result).

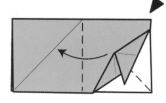

9 Fold the right flap to the left, squashing the flap open. This is easier than it may look, so persevere.

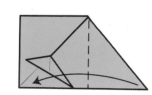

10 Fold the right flap over to the left.

11 Turn the paper over, rotate 45 degrees, and fold the lower corner to the top (uppermost layer only). (The diagrams now show an enlarged view of the model.)

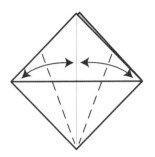

12 Fold both lower edges to the center vertical, crease firmly, and unfold.

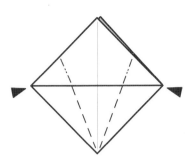

13 Inside reverse fold both flaps on the creases.

At this stage, you are beginning to turn the 2D piece of folded paper into a 3D model. You will probably find it easier to make the inside reverse folds in step 13 if you lift the model up off the table. Open out the top of the paper with one hand while you push in the sides with the other. This photo shows the opposite side of the model from the diagram; you can see the shark's fin.

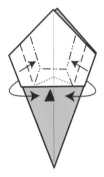

14 Put your fingers in the mouth and carefully form the head of the model into 3D using the creases indicated.

In step 14, use a thumb to push in the paper at the base of the jaw, while squeezing the sides of the mouth.

Continue refining the creases around the jaw, folding the sides of the head flat against the sides of the jaw.

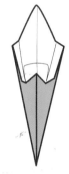

15 This is the result.

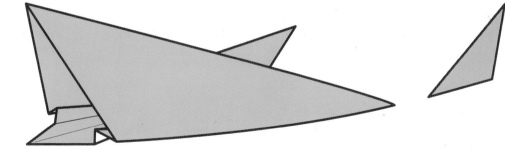

16 Turn over and add a tail fin.

SEE ALSO

Inside reverse fold, page 20
Rabbit's ear, page 23
Squash, page 24

Modular cube

This cube was designed by Francis Ow, a talented geometric designer from Singapore. He has taken the familiar windmill base and, with a few extra creases, turned it into an original and clever design. This type of design is known as "modular" folding and each unit is a "module." It is important to fold neatly so that the units lock tightly into each other and the shape holds together well. It is generally a good idea to have opposite faces of the cube made from the same color.

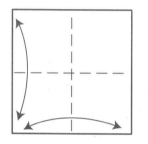

1 Start with a square, white side up. Fold in half both ways, edge to edge. Crease and unfold.

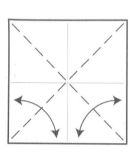

2 Crease and then unfold both diagonals.

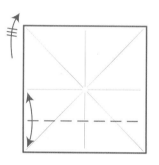

3 Fold the lower edge to the center, crease, and unfold. Repeat on the other three sides.

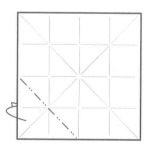

4 Mountain fold the lower left corner behind to the center of the paper.

5 Fold the bottom center corner over. The crease forms a diagonal within the 2x1 creased rectangle.

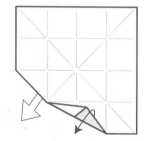

6 Unfold all the creases to get back to the square.

7 This is the result. Repeat steps 4–6 at the three remaining corners.

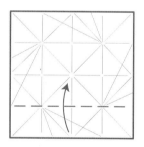

8 Refold the lower edge to the center on a quarter crease mark.

9 Make a kind of rabbit's ear at the lower left corner.

The rabbit's ear formed in step 9 will look the same as a single corner of a windmill base.

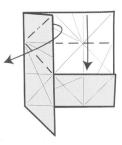

▲ **10** Repeat step 9 at the top left corner.

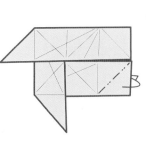

▲ **11** Fold the lower right corner behind.

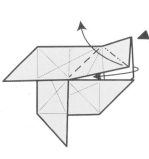

▲ **12** Open and squash the top right corner, folding the white flap over inside. The lower right corner will pop out (see next diagram).

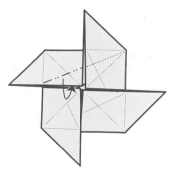

▲ **13** The result is a windmill base. Fold a flap inside, using an existing crease.

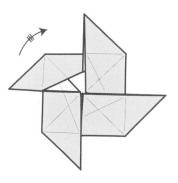

▲ **14** Moving clockwise around the model, repeat on the three remaining sides.

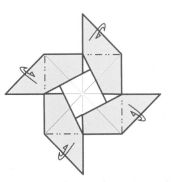

▲ **15** Crease each of the triangular flaps behind, then return them about halfway. The unit is complete. Make five more units, so that you have two each of three different colors.

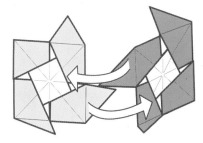

▲ **16** Join two units by wrapping a triangular flap from each unit around each other.

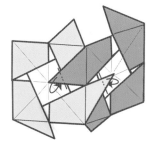

▲ **17** Fold back the tip of each flap to lock the two pieces together.

In step 17, make sure that you tuck in the tip of the flaps as tightly as possible so that the two pieces are securely locked together.

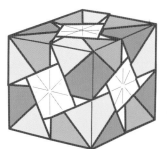

▲ **18** Add the other units in the same way to complete the cube.

Keep tucking in the tips of the flaps tightly for a neat result.

SEE ALSO

Rabbit's ear, page 23
Squash, page 24
Windmill base, page 31

Narrow box

This design is a development by Dennis Walker of work in the 1960s by Giuseppe Baggi. Dennis has extended a simpler box to include a white lip around the edges. The diagrams show a rectangle of letter-size (A4) proportions, but you can make a box from almost any rectangle; a cube variation is also shown. The long box is ideal for presenting candles as gifts. The width of the paper should be a little more than four times that of the candle; it should be the length of the candle, plus just over half the length again. Use a crisp paper to make this box.

1 Start with a rectangle of paper, white side up, creased in half between the long edges. Fold the top and bottom long edges to the center, crease, and unfold.

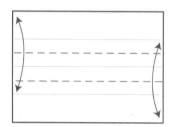

2 Fold the top and bottom edges to the opposite quarter crease. Crease firmly and unfold. This produces the inside $3/8$ creases.

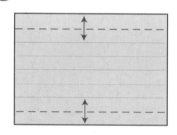

3 Turn the paper over and add the outside $1/8$ creases by folding the top and bottom edges over to the quarter crease marks.

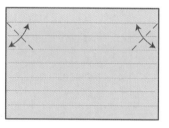

4 Fold the left side so that it lies on the top $1/8$ crease. Make a diagonal crease between the top $1/8$ and $3/8$ creases. Repeat at the top right side.

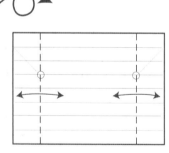

5 Turn back to the white side and add vertical creases that pass through the circled intersection of creases.

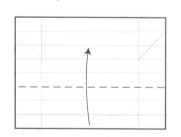

6 Fold the lower edge upward along the bottom $3/8$ crease.

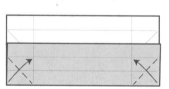

7 Fold the two lower corners over to meet the vertical creases.

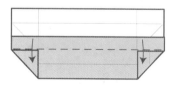

8 Fold down a $1/8$ flap. This will partially cover the triangular flaps.

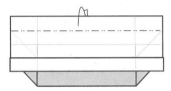

9 Mountain fold the upper ⅛ flap behind.

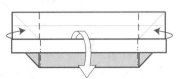

10 Open the model into 3D using the creases indicated. Pinch the vertical edges to help it stay in shape.

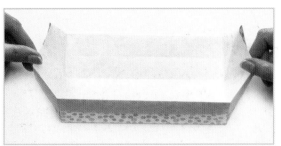

To open the model into 3D in step 10, take hold of each side and simply move them inward, allowing the front edge to open out toward you.

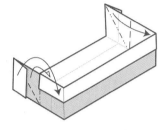

11 Raise the back edges using existing creases.

As you raise the edges in step 11, allow the extra paper at the sides to pleat neatly.

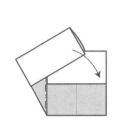

12 Wrap the white "lip" of the back piece around the outside of the layers at each end of the box.

You will find that wrapping the lip in step 12 becomes neater with practice.

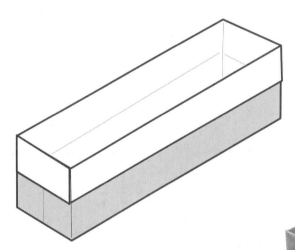

13 The finished box.

▶ **Cube variation** This diagram shows how to precrease the rectangle to produce a cube-shaped box. Crease as shown, then continue the main sequence from step 6 onward.

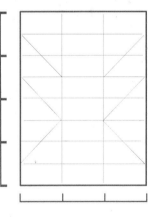

◀ The finished cube variation.

Face lift

I designed this as a fun game that allows you to produce many different faces by folding flaps back and forth. The method of decorating the model is explained in step 15 but, if you are feeling ambitious, you could number all exposed flaps and then unfold the model. You can then cut square pictures into quarters and stick them on the numbered flaps, allowing the model to display images instead of faces. My thanks to the late Dorothy Engleman for suggesting the name.

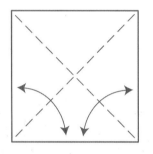

▲ **1** Start with a square, white side up. Crease and unfold both diagonals.

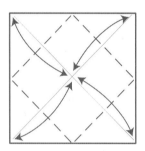

▲ **2** Fold each corner to the center, crease, and unfold.

▲ **3** Fold each corner to the nearest intersection of creases.

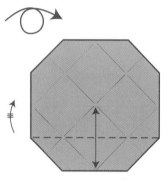

▲ **4** Turn the paper over. Fold the lower edge to the center, crease, and unfold. Repeat at the other three edges.

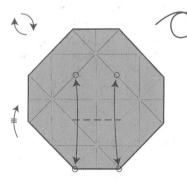

▲ **5** Rotate the paper 45 degrees to this position. Fold the two lower corners to meet creases where circled. Repeat at each edge.

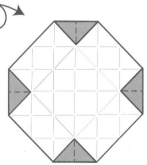

▲ **6** Turn the paper over. Refold the diagonals to pass the valley creases through the colored flaps.

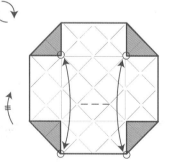

▲ **7** Rotate the paper 45 degrees to this position. Fold the lower corners to the circled points, creasing in the center where indicated only. Repeat at each edge.

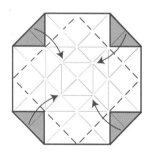

▲ **8** Fold the corners in using existing creases.

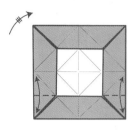

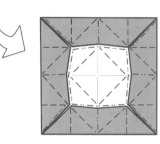

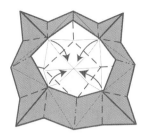

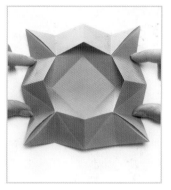

9 Fold the lower edge to the center, creasing only where indicated. Repeat at the other three edges.

10 OK, take a deep breath. All these creases should now be in place, so gently press the corners toward the center, encouraging the paper to open into 3D. (The diagrams now show an enlarged view of the model.)

11 Here is the move in progress. Take your time; all the creases will eventually fall into place.

While performing steps 10 and 11, keep checking that the matching creases on each side are identical.

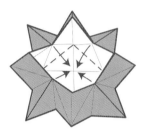

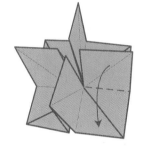

12 This shows how each inside corner will meet in the center of the model. Make sure that the folds in the central white section are correct.

As the corners gradually come together in step 12, you will be left with four square flaps pointing vertically upward.

13 This should be the result. The model is still 3D and should be symmetrical. Fold one flap downward.

As you start folding the flaps down in step 13, you will begin to see how the model works, with each flap providing two sides onto which you can draw the sections of a face.

14 Fold the same flap upward. Repeat with the other three flaps, folding them each way and leaving the paper more or less flat when you have finished.

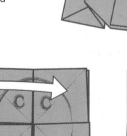

15 Draw a face, then fold a flap over and add a different shape to join the existing sections of the face. Fold all flaps both ways to make sure every possibility is completed.

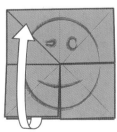

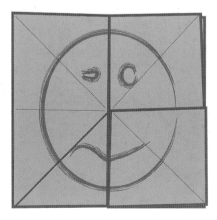

T-Rex

American Marc Kirschenbaum is best known for his more complex designs, but he has also created several simple ones. This T-Rex has a folding sequence that is clearly defined, with reference points for every fold except the very last step, which you fold to suit your own tastes. This means you can produce the same results every time and virtually nothing is left to chance. This type of model is perfect for beginners because it only uses valley and mountain folds—no sinks or reverses.

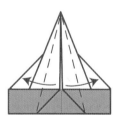

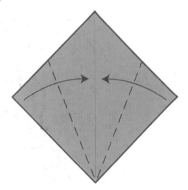

▲ **1** Start with a square, white side up. Crease a diagonal and unfold. Turn the paper over and fold the two lower edges to the center crease to form a kite base.

▲ **2** Fold a colored edge to the horizontal edge and make a pinch to mark the center.

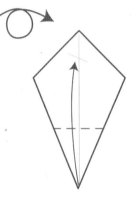

▲ **3** Turn the paper over and fold the lower point up to the pinch mark.

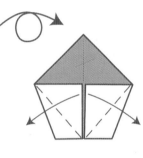

▲ **4** Turn the paper over. Fold out the inner corners as far as you can.

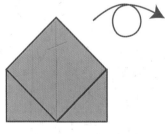

▲ **5** This is the result. Turn the paper over.

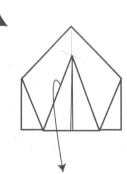

▲ **6** Unfold the narrow central flap.

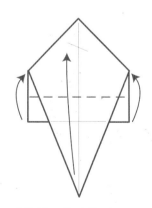

▲ **7** Fold so that the lower right-angled corners meet the corners above them. The bottom point will fold up again at the same time.

▲ **8** Fold the central flaps out as far as they will go.

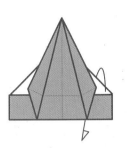 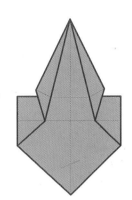 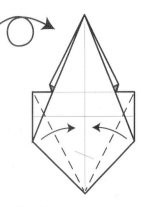 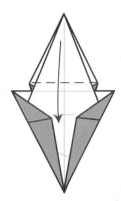

9 Fold down the flap from underneath.

10 This is the result.

11 Turn the paper over and fold the lower sides in—the creases will connect the lower point with the upper right-angled corners.

12 Fold the upper flap down on a crease that connects the corners of the upper white raw edges.

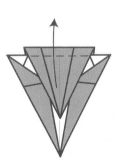 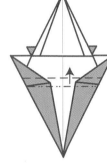  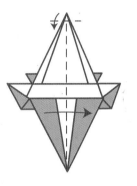 

13 Fold the flap upward—the crease should lie on an existing crease on the paper underneath.

14 Fold the lower flap upward on an existing crease, then fold it back down to form a small pleat.

In step 14, you are forming a pleat to mark the end of the body and the start of the tail.

15 Fold the top point over (this is the tip of the nose), then fold the model in half from left to right.

By the end of step 15, you can clearly see the shape of the dinosaur.

  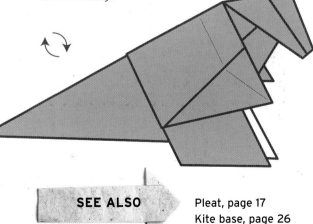

16 Fold the head over at a suitable angle.

The angle at which you fold the head in step 16 can vary.

17 Rotate the finished dinosaur so that it stands on its hindlegs.

SEE ALSO   Pleat, page 17
Kite base, page 26

Mouse behind cheese

It is rare to find an origami design that is (intentionally) humorous. This is one of my regular explorations into this area. The design is part of a series that includes "dog behind tree," "bear climbing tree," and other little known classics. It is also an interesting example of how a few creases can turn a 2D sheet of paper into a 3D illusion. In fact, this design started life as a much simpler "lump of cheese."

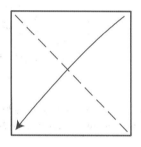

▲ **1** Start with a square, cheese color downward. Fold on one diagonal.

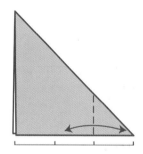

▲ **2** Fold the lower right corner over about one third of the way along the raw edge. Crease and unfold.

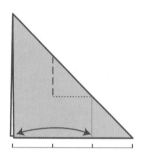

▲ **3** Fold the vertical edge to meet this crease, but do not crease any lower than the top of the previous crease. Unfold.

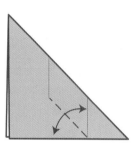

▲ **4** Make a crease joining the bottom points of the two vertical creases, then unfold.

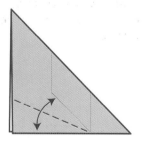

▲ **5** Fold the lower edge to meet the most recent crease, then unfold.

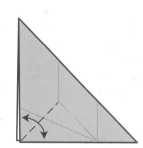

▲ **6** Crease from the lower left corner to the corner of the diamond-shaped area. Unfold.

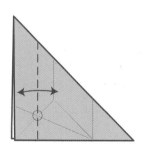

▲ **7** Make a vertical crease that passes through the lower intersection of creases. Note that the left edge will not align with the nearest vertical crease. Unfold.

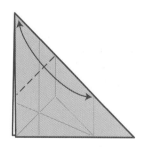

▲ **8** Fold the top corner over to lie along the folded edge. The crease starts where the central vertical crease meets the folded edge. Unfold.

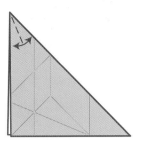

9 Fold the tip of the upper corner in half, creasing a short distance, then unfold.

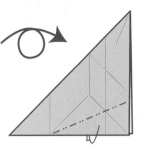

10 Turn the paper over. The precreasing is complete, so you can now start folding the model into shape. Fold the uppermost layer of the bottom right corner inside.

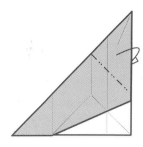

11 Fold the upper section of the triangle behind.

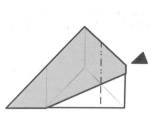

12 Inside reverse fold the right-hand section.

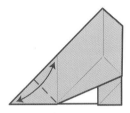

13 Fold the lower left corner to meet the nearest crease, then unfold.

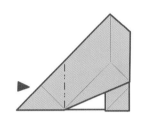

14 Make another inside reverse fold.

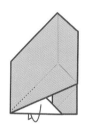

15 Tuck the white triangle inside, using the crease made in step 13.

In step 15, you are tucking the white triangle inside the model.

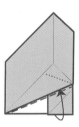

16 Fold the lower right corner, tucking it into the small pocket.

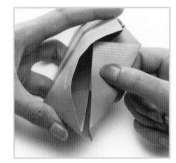

Tucking in the lower right corner in step 16 completes the shape of the cheese.

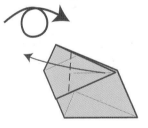

17 Turn the model over and fold the narrow flap over. The exact distance is not important, but the lower edge of the flap should pass through the center left corner.

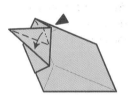

18 Fold the tail in half, squashing as needed on the upper side.

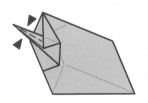

19 Further squash the tail into a narrow point.

Define the point of the mouse's tail to complete the illusion.

20 Turn the model back over to complete the design.

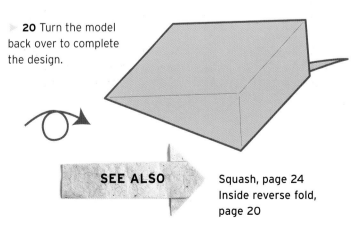

SEE ALSO

Squash, page 24
Inside reverse fold, page 20

Wentworth bowl

I had the basis for this design lying in my "possibles" box for over a year, but could not find a way to make it hold together satisfactorily. In a moment of inspiration, I decided to blintz the paper (fold all corners to the center), then try again. It quickly and almost instinctively fell into place. Some designs almost seem to lie hidden in the paper, waiting for someone to discover them.

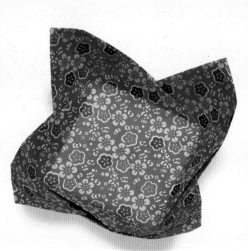

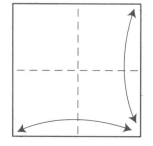

▲ **1** Start with a square, white side up. Fold in half both ways, crease, and unfold.

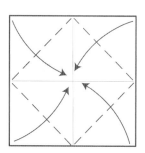

▲ **2** Fold all four corners to the center.

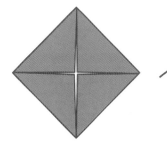

▲ **3** The result is a blintz base. Turn the paper over.

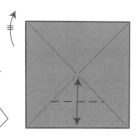

▲ **4** Rotate to this position. Fold the lower edge to the center, creasing only between the existing crease lines. Unfold and repeat on the three other sides. (The diagrams now show an enlarged view of the model.)

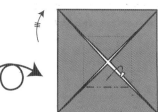

▶ **6** Turn back over and fold the lower left corner to the center, creasing only the indicated section of the paper. Unfold and repeat on the other three sides.

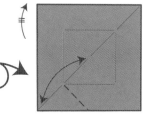

▲ **5** Turn the paper over and tuck the four corners underneath.

▲ **7** Fold this recent crease to the quarter crease (see also next diagram).

▲ **8** Use the circled points as guidance and only crease where shown. Unfold again and repeat on the other three sides.

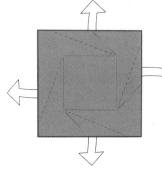

▲ **9** Unfold the corners from underneath.

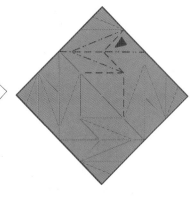

▲ **10** Use the indicated creases to form one side of the bowl.

Follow step 10 to form the first side of the bowl.

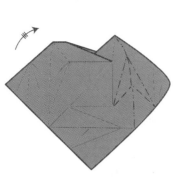

△ **11** Form the second side of the bowl and continue with the other two.

The second side being formed. It is best to form all four sides of the bowl before working on the base.

△ **12** Turn the paper over and fold an edge underneath on an existing crease.

△ **13** Fold in again. Tuck the flap inside all the layers to hold it in place.

△ **14** Repeat on the three other sides.

Tuck in the flaps on the underside of the bowl, as instructed in steps 13 and 14.

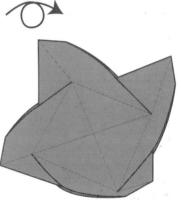

△ **15** Turn over for the completed bowl. Use a thumb and forefinger to encourage a curve on the long edges.

VARIATION

△ **1** Fold steps 1–5 of the main sequence. Turn over and fold the lower left corner to lie on a quarter crease.

△ **2** Crease the indicated section of the paper, then unfold.

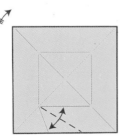

▷ **3** Fold this recent crease to the quarter crease. Crease where indicated, then unfold. Repeat on the other three sides, then continue from step 9 of the main sequence.

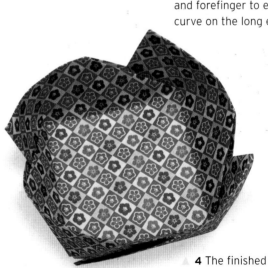

△ **4** The finished bowl variation.

SEE ALSO Blintz base, page 27

Pipe

Created by Ted Megrath from the UK, this is a wonderful design to have in your repertoire—people are delighted to receive one as a gift and it takes just a few minutes to fold once you have learned it. Ted himself does not worry about the first nine steps and instead just forms a tube and squashes it—give it a try if you are feeling adventurous. Forming the bowl in step 15 needs some care if you want a neat result.

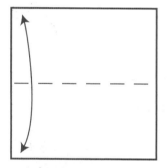

▲ **1** Start with a square of paper, white side up. Fold in half from top to bottom, crease, and unfold.

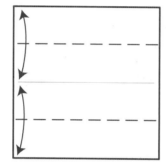

▲ **2** Fold upper and lower edges to the center crease, then unfold.

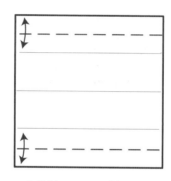

▲ **3** Fold upper and lower edges to the quarter creases, then unfold.

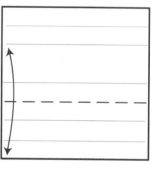

▲ **4** Fold the lower edge to the upper quarter crease, then unfold.

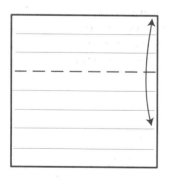

▲ **5** Fold the upper edge to the lower quarter crease, then unfold.

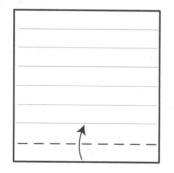

▲ **6** Fold the lower edge over on the first crease.

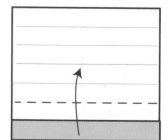

▲ **7** Fold the lower edge over on the second crease.

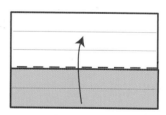

▲ **8** Fold over along the colored folded edge.

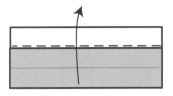

9 Again, fold over along the colored folded edge.

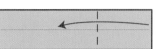

10 Fold the right short edge over about a third of the way across.

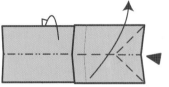

11 Fold over a small strip of the upper section, crease firmly, and unfold.

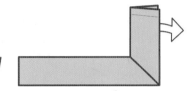

12 Fold the lower edge of the uppermost section of paper to meet the vertical right-hand edge. Crease as far as the horizontal center crease, then unfold.

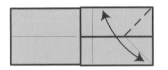

13 Repeat step 12 on the upper edge of the uppermost section of paper.

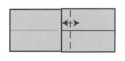
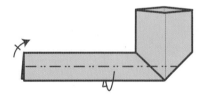

14 Mountain fold the bottom section of paper in half. At the same time, valley fold the uppermost section in half, pressing in on the diagonal creases you have just made.

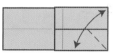

15 Carefully ease out the layers of the uppermost section to form the bowl of the pipe.

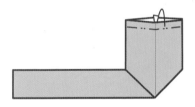

16 Fold a lip all the way around the bowl, tucking the paper into the center of the bowl.

17 Mountain fold the topmost layer of paper, tucking it into the center of the stem. Repeat on the other side.

When opening out the layers in step 15, put a finger inside to help. When you have finished, you will clearly see the bowl and stem of the pipe beginning to form in 3D.

18 Squeeze the end of the stem together as you press it to the right—see the final drawing. Widen the bowl of the pipe by pressing where indicated.

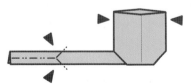

In step 18, simultaneously squeeze the tip of the pipe stem as you press it to the right.

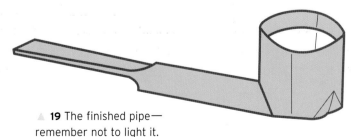

19 The finished pipe—remember not to light it.

Locked box

Many paper folders have a fascination with boxes and containers. The challenge is to make them secure, so that they stay in shape. If you look at the corners of this design of mine, you can see that it would be impossible to tuck the corner inside at the end of the folding because it is a right-angled corner. So, each corner is flattened so that the tucking in can be done easily.

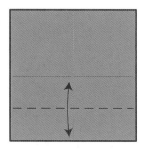

1 Start with a square, colored side up. Crease in half from side to side, both ways. Fold one edge to the center, crease, and unfold. Repeat on the three other sides.

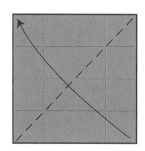

2 Fold in half diagonally.

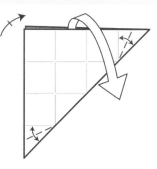

3 Make a bisecting crease on the triangular sections at each end of the folded edge. Open the paper out and then repeat on the other diagonal.

4 Make a crease that starts at the lower left intersection of the quarter creases. Fold so that the circled points meet.

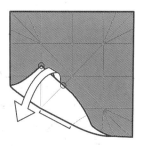

5 Crease only where shown, then unfold.

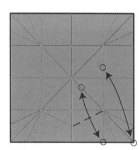

6 Repeat the same fold from the lower right edge.

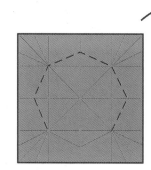

7 Repeat this fold around the remaining edges and corners, as indicated.

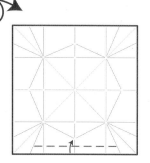

8 Turn the paper over and fold the lower edge in to meet the nearest intersection of creases. Extend the crease only as far as indicated.

9 Make a crease at 45 degrees as shown, then unfold. Repeat the move on each side.

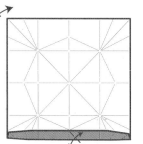

10 Here is an enlarged view of a corner. Fold the corner in.

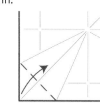

11 Fold both layers over, making a crease between the next two nearest creases. Crease (a small corner will be doubled over) and unfold. Repeat at each corner.

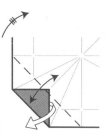

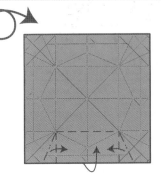

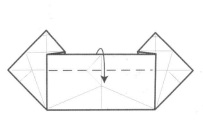

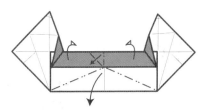

14 Fold the paper inside using the mountain creases, allowing a small crimp to form in the center.

12 Turn the paper over to the colored side. Raise one side using the creases indicated (you may have to "swap" some from mountain to valley and vice versa).

13 Fold the edge down. Crease it all the way along, including the end sections inside the curved paper leading to the corners. Do not worry about flattening the ends just yet.

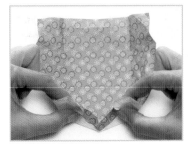

This is a view from above of the crimp formed in step 14.

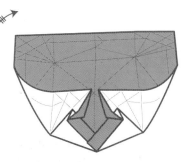

16 With any luck, this will be the result. Fold each of the loose corners outward.

The corners should flatten naturally when you fold them outward in step 16.

15 Press the completed creases firmly so that they stay in place, then repeat steps 12–14 on each side. You may find it easier to make these folds with the paper "in the air," holding it gently.

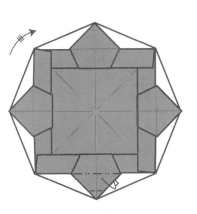

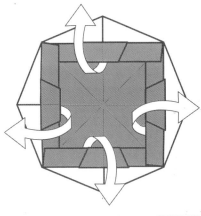

18 Carefully unfold the sides.

The final stage is to pinch the corners and edges to neaten the shape of the box.

17 Tuck each of the corners neatly underneath the colored rim, using existing creases.

19 Pinch through the major creases so the box will stay in shape.

SEE ALSO   Crimp, page 22

Boat with keel

This boat by Martin Wall of the UK is an ingenious design. It uses a logical sequence of folds that opens into a fully three-dimensional design at the very end. At step 18, you can see the familiar sequence of the waterbomb base taking place. Origami moves and sequences are often reused on a smaller scale as you progress through a design.

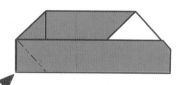

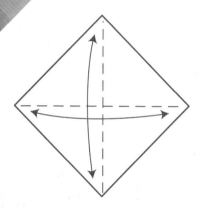

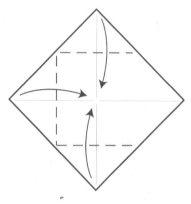

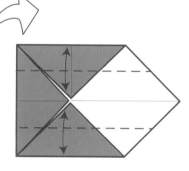

▲ **1** Start with a square, white side up. Fold in half diagonally both ways, then unfold.

▲ **2** Fold three corners to the center.

▲ **3** Fold upper and lower edges to the center horizontal, crease, and unfold. (The diagrams now show an enlarged view of the model.)

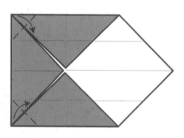

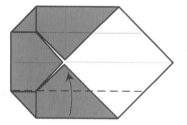

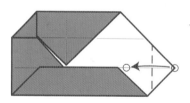

▲ **4** Fold the upper and lower left corners in to meet the creases made in step 3.

▲ **5** Refold the lower quarter to the center.

▲ **6** Fold the right corner to the left, stopping just short of the inner colored corner.

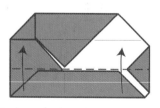

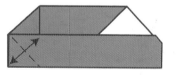

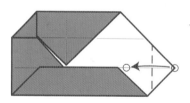

▲ **7** Now fold the lower section over again.

▲ **8** Fold the lower left corner to the center horizontal, crease firmly, then unfold.

▲ **9** Now inside reverse fold the same corner.

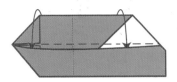

▲ **10** Fold the upper half inside the lower half, trapping the small triangular layer on the left. The left end will form the front of the boat; the right end will form the keel.

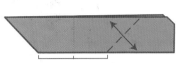

▲ **11** Imagine a point the same distance from the vertical crease as the front corner. Fold the rear flap over at 45 degrees at this point, crease, and unfold.

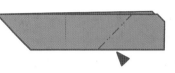

▲ **12** Inside reverse fold the flap on the same crease.

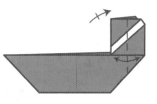

▲ **13** Fold the top layer of the vertical flap in half from right to left, then unfold. Repeat on the layer underneath.

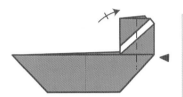

▲ **14** Inside reverse fold the same flaps on either side.

In step 14, the boat begins to open out into a 3D model, with the keel pointing upward.

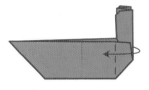

▲ **15** Open out the rear flap evenly.

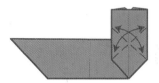

▲ **16** Make two creases at 45 degrees to the vertical.

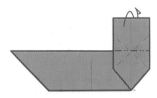

▲ **17** Fold the upper half behind, crease, and unfold.

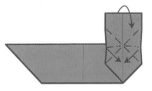

▲ **18** Collapse the flap over to the front to form a waterbomb base shape.

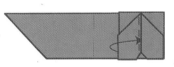

▲ **19** Fold the left flap over, tucking it into a pocket on the right.

Tuck in the left flap neatly in step 19.

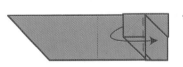

▲ **20** Swing the remaining flap from left to right.

▲ **21** Make these valley creases on both sides.

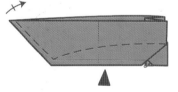

▲ **22** Open the boat, adding a gentle curved crease to shape the sides. Fold the lower corner of the keel between the layers.

Gently press the base of the boat upward to form the curved shape as you open out the boat in step 22.

▲ **23** The finished boat.

 **SEE ALSO**

Inside reverse fold, page 20
Waterbomb base, page 30

Wild goat

This design is by Robert Lang of the United States. Over the course of many years he has proved himself not only to be a master of origami techniques, but also a folder of great sensitivity, giving his models a life that is hard even for excellent folders to recapture. It is recommended that you start with a large square for your first attempts; when you have mastered the sequence, you can fold from smaller sheets.

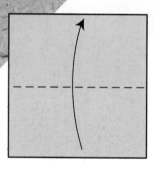

▲ **1** Start with a square, colored side up. Fold in half.

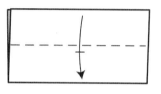

▲ **2** Fold the uppermost raw edge down to the folded edge. Repeat underneath.

▲ **3** Fold the uppermost right-hand edge over to the lower edge. Repeat underneath.

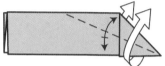

▲ **4** Fold the uppermost right edge to the lower edge. Crease. Unfold this and the previous fold. Repeat underneath.

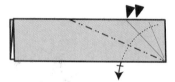

▲ **5** Inside reverse fold both top right corners on the most recent creases.

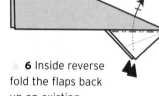

▲ **6** Inside reverse fold the flaps back up on existing creases.

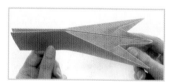

▲ **7** Inside reverse fold the remaining flaps back inside.

The result of all the reverse folding after completing step 7.

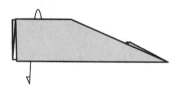

▲ **8** Open out the piece by swinging the underneath section downward.

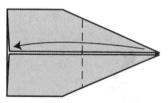

▲ **9** Fold the narrow point to the opposite end.

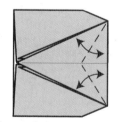

▲ **10** Fold each side of the triangular point to the right edge, crease, and unfold.

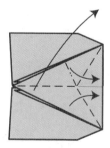

▲ **11** Make a rabbit's ear on the flap (see next diagram for result).

▷ **12** Fold the top section down behind, leaving the rabbit's ear where it is.

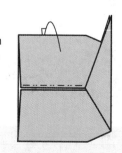

▷ **13** Fold the left edge to the inside folded edge, crease, and unfold.

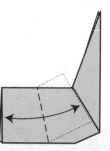

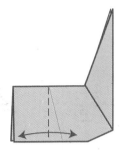

14 Fold the same edge over at right angles to the horizontal. The crease should pass through the top of the most recent crease.

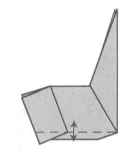

15 Form an inside crimp, using existing creases.

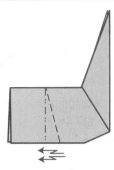

16 Valley fold through all layers, starting at the lower right corner.

17 Fold a small flap of the uppermost layer inside.

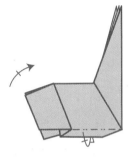

18 Fold the remainder inside. Repeat underneath.

Tuck the lower edges inside. This gives the goat a straight edge on which to stand.

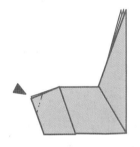

19 Sink the back corner to round the rear of the animal.

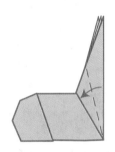

20 Fold the top two layers on the right over to the left, allowing the layers inside to open.

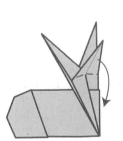

21 Flatten the central flap symmetrically.

The flap you are manipulating in step 21 will form the face of the goat.

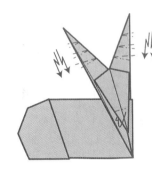

22 Fold the tip of the nose underneath. Make a series of inside crimps to form the horns.

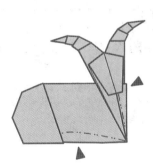

23 Sink the central corner on the right and shape the belly of the animal.

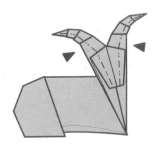

24 Make gentle mountain creases on the head and horns to form them into 3D.

25 The finished wild goat.

SEE ALSO

Inside reverse fold, page 20
Inside crimp, page 22
Rabbit's ear, page 23
Sink, page 25

Sentinel bird

This design makes use of the traditional stretched bird base, a development of the preliminary base. Here, it is used by creator Jeff Beynon to make a bird, but this base is very flexible and can be used for many subjects. The techniques used to create the head and beak will be invaluable in your origami development, so pay careful attention to them. Several of these folds have no exact location, so you should determine their position using your imagination and artistic judgment.

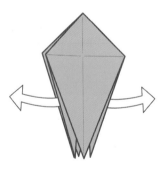

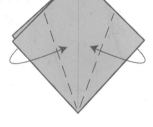 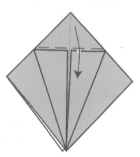 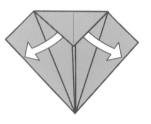 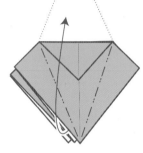

1 Start with a preliminary base, with the color outward and the original corners of the square at the bottom. Fold the two lower edges up to the vertical center crease (uppermost layer only).

2 Fold over the triangular flap at the top.

3 Unfold the two flaps from beneath the triangular flap.

4 Fold up the first layer at the bottom, using the upper edge as a hinge.

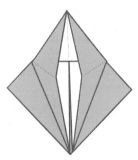 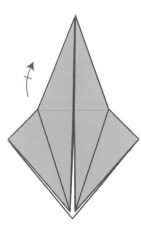 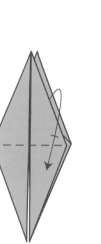

5 This shows the fold in progress.

6 Here it is complete. Repeat steps 4–5 on the other side.

7 Fold the topmost upper flap down to the bottom, then repeat the move underneath.

8 This is the bird base. Carefully hold the hidden central flaps on either side and start to ease them apart.

9 This is the move in progress—check you are making the creases shown, and keep pulling apart.

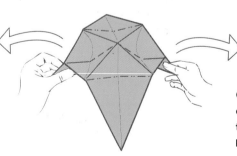

Continue pulling the central flaps apart to stretch the bird base in step 9.

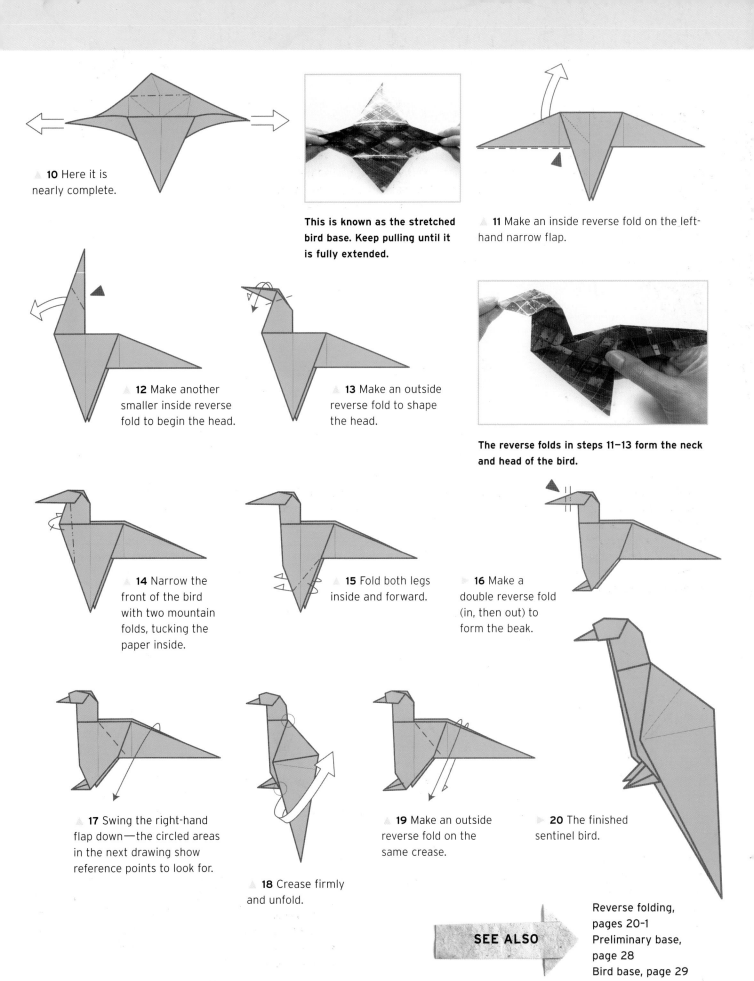

10 Here it is nearly complete.

This is known as the stretched bird base. Keep pulling until it is fully extended.

11 Make an inside reverse fold on the left-hand narrow flap.

12 Make another smaller inside reverse fold to begin the head.

13 Make an outside reverse fold to shape the head.

The reverse folds in steps 11–13 form the neck and head of the bird.

14 Narrow the front of the bird with two mountain folds, tucking the paper inside.

15 Fold both legs inside and forward.

16 Make a double reverse fold (in, then out) to form the beak.

17 Swing the right-hand flap down—the circled areas in the next drawing show reference points to look for.

18 Crease firmly and unfold.

19 Make an outside reverse fold on the same crease.

20 The finished sentinel bird.

SEE ALSO

Reverse folding, pages 20-1
Preliminary base, page 28
Bird base, page 29

Skunk

This is one of my own designs, and has clean lines and a lively attitude. The tail is formed in step 12 using a three-dimensional sink that looks complex, but only requires care and accurate creasing. Since it is 3D, you will not be able to complete the move with the paper flat on the table; it needs to be held in the air. If you gently collapse the paper, checking that all the creases match the drawings, you will succeed.

1 Start with a square, colored side up, that has a diagonal crease. Fold one corner to both nearest corners, creasing only as far as the center diagonal.

2 Turn the paper over and fold the raw edges to the creases made in step 1. Crease and unfold.

3 Turn the paper over again. Add the creases indicated by folding the creases made in step 1 to the center of the paper.

4 Fold the top corner to the center, crease, and unfold.

5 Turn the paper over and collapse the paper using the creases indicated.

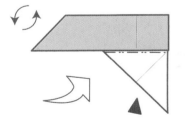

6 Rotate the paper to this position. Inside reverse fold the lower flap. (The diagrams now show an enlarged view of the model.)

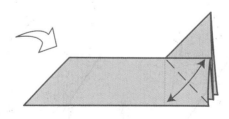

7 Fold the corner in half on a diagonal crease, then unfold.

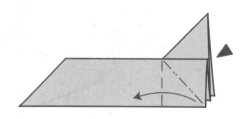

8 Make a squash fold on the corner.

The squash fold in step 8 is the first stage of forming the hindlegs of the skunk.

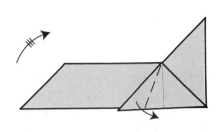

9 Fold the edge of the triangular flap to the vertical crease. Repeat this and steps 7–8 on the underside.

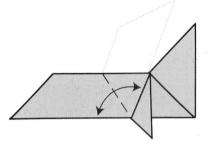

10 The left end will form the tail. Fold the tail over so that it lies on a folded edge, crease firmly, and unfold.

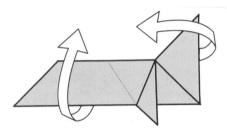

11 Open the model from underneath, but not completely—leave the creases in place.

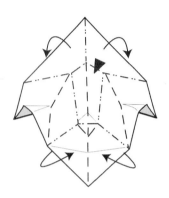

12 Reform the creases using the pattern indicated and collapse the paper along them. This sinks the center point of the paper and forms the tail.

Collapsing the paper in step 12 is not as tricky as it looks, provided you go slowly.

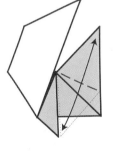

13 Fold the tip of the front flap down to the end of the hindleg. Crease and unfold.

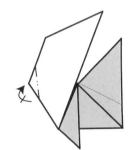

14 Fold a small flap of the tail inside, repeating underneath.

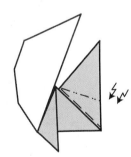

15 Shape the head with an outside crimp, tucking the crimped paper into the pockets on either side of the front leg.

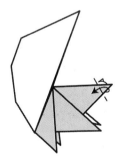

16 Outside reverse fold the tip of the nose.

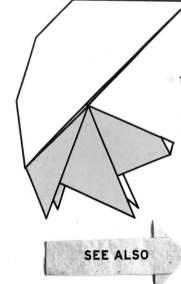

17 The finished skunk.

SEE ALSO

Inside and outside reverse folds, page 20
Outside crimp, page 22
Squash, page 24

Around the houses

This is a collaborative design produced by myself and Mick Guy. The concept is borrowed from a puzzle called "edge matching," where you arrange nine pieces so that patterns on every edge match with each other. It is great fun to try, but also fiendishly difficult, so here is a clue—one of the modules with opposing triangles and rectangles is in the center of the solution. Good luck. You will need four different colors of paper, each with white on the other side.

RECTANGLE UNIT

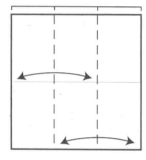

▲ **1** Start with a square, white side up, that has been creased in half and unfolded. Fold into thirds, then unfold.

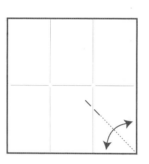

▲ **2** Fold the lower edge to meet the right-hand edge, making a pinch mark on the one-third crease. Unfold.

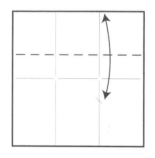

▲ **3** Fold the upper edge to meet the pinch mark. Crease and unfold.

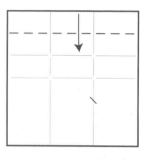

▲ **4** Fold the upper edge to the most recent crease.

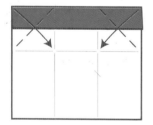

▲ **5** Fold the edges in to lie on the original halfway crease.

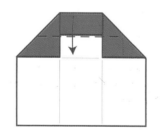

▲ **6** Fold the top section down to the halfway crease.

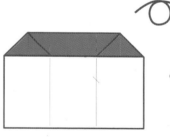

7 This is the result. Turn the paper over.

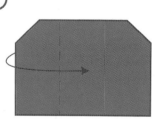

▲ **8** Fold the left side over on a one-third crease.

▶ **9** Fold the right side over the top of it.

Step 9 in progress. The folding sequence for the unit is easy to follow.

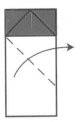

10 Fold the lower white section to lie along the bottom of the colored section.

Step 10 completes the folding of the first unit.

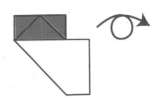

11 This is the underside of the rectangle unit. Turn over.

12 This is the top of the rectangle unit. Fold four units in total from red paper, six from blue, four from yellow, and four from green.

TRIANGLE UNIT

13 Starting with the square colored side up, follow steps 1–4 of the rectangle unit. Unfold, then fold the top corners in to the first crease.

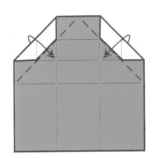

14 Fold them over again on a diagonal crease.

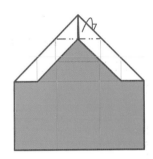

15 Fold once more in the same way.

16 Mountain fold the top triangle behind.

Step 16 starts the shaping of the top of the unit.

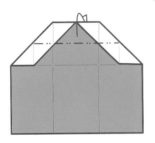

17 Fold the next section behind also.

Step 17 completes the shaping. Again, the folding sequence for this unit is very easy.

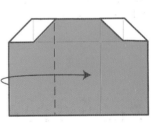

18 Fold the left-hand section to the right.

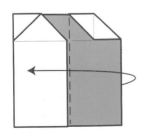

19 Fold the right-hand section to the left.

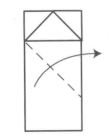

20 Fold the lower flap over as before.

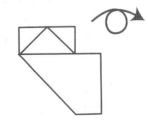

21 This is the underside of the triangle unit. Turn over.

22 This is the top of the triangle unit. Fold five units in total from red paper, three from blue, five from yellow, and five from green.

ASSEMBLY

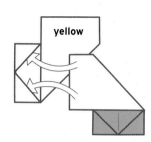

Slot two units together in step 23 by slipping the white flap into the pockets.

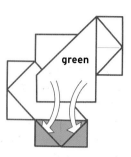

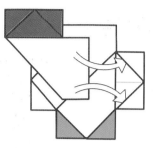

▲ **23** Start with a yellow triangle and blue rectangle, face down, arranged as shown. Slide the white flap of the blue rectangle into the pockets on the back of the yellow triangle.

▲ **24** Slide the white flap of a green triangle into the pockets of the blue rectangle.

▲ **25** Slide the white flap of a red rectangle into the pockets of the green triangle.

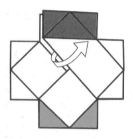

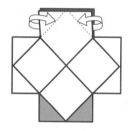

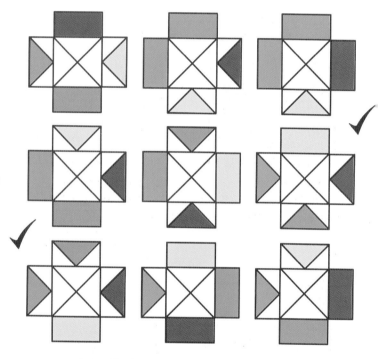

▲ **26** Pull out the white flap from below the red rectangle and slide the red section underneath it.

▲ **27** Tuck the white flap into the pockets on the back of the red rectangle.

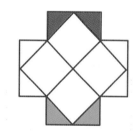

Finish joining the four sections to complete the unit in step 27.

▲ **28** This is the result.

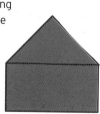

▲ **Playing** Try to arrange the shapes so that every colored rectangle has a matching colored triangle next to it, forming the shape of a house. The aim is to get 12 houses in total. The 12 colored sections around the outside of the pattern do not matter—they can be any color. In the example shown here, only the upper right (yellow) and lower left (blue) units match properly to form houses.

This is a house

▶ **29** Turn the paper over to reveal the first complete puzzle unit, matching the top left unit in the playing example. Assemble the other colors and patterns in the same way to match the remaining puzzle units. Be careful.

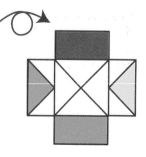

SEE ALSO

Fold equal amounts, pages 18–19

Welsh corgi

This design by Guspath Go from Hong Kong is as complex as you will find in this book, so it has been placed at the end as a challenge. It may take several attempts to complete, but you will get there in the end. The first nine steps are precreasing, so just fold slowly and neatly. The other tricky steps are the initial forming of the tail in step 15 and the finish of the tail. Persevere—you will learn a great deal by mastering these steps.

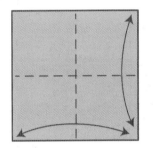

1 Start with a square, colored side up. Crease in half both ways and unfold.

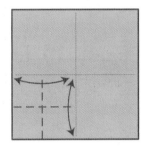

2 Fold the lower left quarter section in half both ways, then unfold.

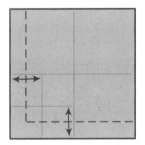

3 Add ⅛ creases on the lower and left sides, creasing only where indicated.

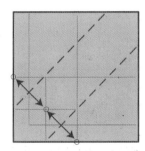

4 Fold the center point of the lower edge to meet the vertical crease indicated. Crease and unfold. Repeat with the center point of the left edge.

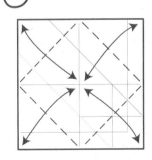

5 Turn over and fold all four corners to the center, crease, and unfold.

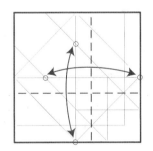

6 Fold the center points of the lower and right edges to meet the circled crease intersections.

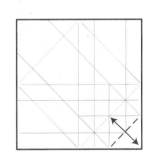

7 Fold the lower right corner to the nearest crease intersection, crease, and unfold.

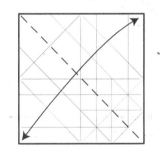

8 Fold the lower left to upper right corner, crease a diagonal, then unfold.

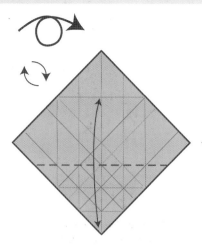

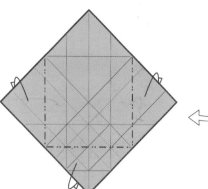

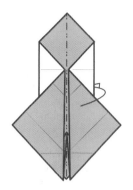

9 Turn back to the colored side and rotate the paper to this position. Fold the lower corner to the upper crease intersection, crease, and unfold.

10 Refold underneath three of the creases made in step 5.

11 Fold the lower edge to the original center. At the same time, fold the left and right sides to the center, allowing the flaps to pop out from underneath.

12 This is the result. Mountain fold in half.

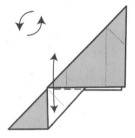

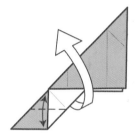

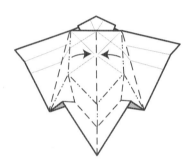

13 Rotate the paper to this position. Fold the lower section upward along the raw edge, crease, then unfold.

14 Crease the lower section in half, then partially unfold the paper underneath.

15 Change the creases indicated so they match this pattern of valleys and mountains. The paper will collapse flat again, if you are careful.

If you match the crease directions shown in step 15, you will find that the model will flatten easily. Paper that is the same color on each side is used here; you may find it easier to use paper that is white on one side for your first try.

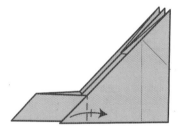

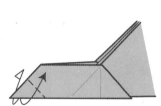

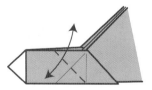

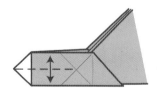

16 Fold the small triangular flap to the right. Repeat on the other side.

17 Make an outside reverse fold on the tip of the tail.

18 Fold the tail to meet the vertical crease. Crease and unfold.

19 Fold the tail in half, creasing as far as the previous crease.

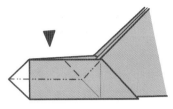

20 Open the top of the tail slightly and start to make these creases. Look at the next diagram as well, which shows the move from above and behind, halfway through.

21 Sink the point near the tip of the tail by applying pressure where shown so that the point is "popped" inside. This is known as a closed sink, which locks the point of the paper inside the sink. The layers underneath will not be symmetrical, but it does not matter which side is thicker.

The tip of the tail being sunk and then the sides flattened in steps 21 and 22.

22 Flatten the tail again using these creases—hold the tail in one hand, the back legs in the other, and gently press them together.

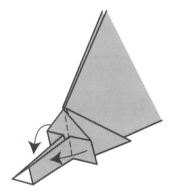

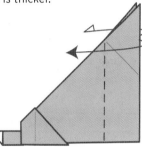

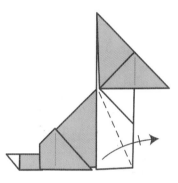

23 This is the result. Fold the loose flaps backward.

24 Using an existing crease, open out all layers, allowing the head to fold forward naturally.

25 Fold the first layer forward on a crease between the back of the head and the lower right corner. Repeat on the other side.

26 Tuck the excess paper inside the model, front and back.

27 Outside reverse fold the tip of the nose.

28 The finished Welsh corgi.

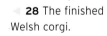

SEE ALSO   Outside reverse fold, page 20
Sink, page 25

Index

A

animals:

Jaws 1 56–9

Jaws 2 94–5

Skunk 118–19

T-Rex 102–3

Welsh Corgi 123–5

Wild Goat 114–15

Around the Houses
120–2

B

Baggi, Giuseppe 98

Banger 50–2

bases 26–31

bird 29

blintz 27

kite 26

multiform 31

preliminary 28

waterbomb 30

windmill 31

Basketball Hoop 46–9

Beynon, Jeff 116

bird base 29

birds:

Penguin 37–9

Sentinel Bird
116–17

"birogami" 53

Blencoe, Philip 53

blintz base 27

boats:

Boat with Keel 112–13

Sailboat 40–1

boxes:

Box with Legs 80–3

Crown variations 63

Gift Box 92–3

Locked Box 110–11

Narrow Box 98–9

Polyhedron variation
63

Sanbow (Box with legs)
80–3

Star Box 64–7

Butterfly 76–9

C

corgi: Welsh Corgi 123–5

creasing 12

crimp 22

Crown 60–2

Box variation 63

Polyhedron variation 63

cube: Modular Cube 96–7

cutting to size 13

D

dog: Welsh Corgi 123–5

double reverse fold 21

drawings: scale 17

E

Engelmann, Dorothy
100

F

Face Lift 100–1

fine-art paper 11

Finger Puppet 53–5

flower: Tulip 68–71

foil paper 11

fold equal amounts
18–19

fold and unfold 16

folding 12–13

creasing 12

crimp 22

double reverse 21

equal amounts 18–19

fold and unfold 16

inside reverse 20

into thirds 18–19

mountain 15

pleat 17

point to point 17

positioning 12

rabbit's ear 23

repeat 16

reverse 20–1

sink 25

squash 24

symbols 14–15

techniques 14–25

tips 13

valley 14

folding bone 12

Fortune-teller 42–5

found paper 11

Fuse, Tomoko 92

G

Gift Box 92–3

Glynn, Robin 92

Go, Guspath 123

goat: Wild Goat 114–15

Guy, Mick 120

I

inside crimp 22

inside reverse fold 20

J

Jaws 1 56–9

Jaws 2 94–5

K

Kirschenbaum, Marc 102

kite base 26

L

Lang, Robert 114–15

Locked Box 110–11

Lucio, Rene 53

M

Megrath, Ted 108

Modular Cube 96–7

money, paper 11

mountain fold 15

    converting to valley

      fold 15

Mouse Behind Cheese

    104–5

multiform base 31

N

Narrow Box 98–9

Ninja Star 84–9

O

orientation: changing 16

origami paper 10

outside crimp 22

outside reverse fold 20

Ow, Francis 96

P

paper:

    creasing 12

    cutting to size 13

    positioning 12

    preparation 12–13

    types 10–11

paper money 11

Penguin 37–9

photocopy paper 10

Pipe 108–9

pleat 17

point to point fold 17

Polyhedron: Crown

    variation 63

positioning 12

preliminary base 28

preparation 12–13

puppet: Finger Puppet 53–5

R

rabbit's ear 23

rectangle: cutting from

    square 13

repeat fold 16

reverse folding 20–1

    double 21

    inside 20

    outside 20

S

Sailboat 40–1

Saltcellar 42

Sanbow (Box with legs)

    80–3

scale: of drawings 17

Sentinel Bird 116–17

shark:

    Jaws 1 56–9

    Jaws 2 94–5

sink 25

Skunk 118–19

square: cutting from

    rectangle 13

squash 24

Star Box 64–7

stars:

    Ninja Star 84–9

    Star Box 64–7

symbols 14–15, 16, 17, 21

T

T-Rex 102–3

techniques 14–25

    changing crease

      direction 15

    changing orientation 16

    creating thirds from

      template 19

    crimp 22

    fold equal amounts 18

    fold point to point 17

    fold and unfold 16

    mountain fold 15

    pleat 17

    rabbit's ear 23

    repeat fold 16

    reverse folding 20–1

    sink 25

    squash 24

    valley fold 14

Temko, Florence 34

thirds: folding into 18–19

Tulip 68–71

V

valley fold 14

    converting to mountain

      fold 15

W

Walker, Dennis 98

Wall, Martin 112

Waterbomb 72–5

waterbomb base 30

Welsh Corgi 123–5

Wentworth Bowl 106–7

Wild Goat 114–15

windmill base 31

Wingding 34–6

wrapping paper 10

Y

Yoshizawa, Akira 76

Credits

Author's acknowledgments

The author takes creative ownership very seriously and has made every effort to trace the source of the designs featured in this book accurately. However, there are many examples in origami of independent creation of apparently similar designs. Our thanks to the following creators for their kind permission to reproduce their work in this book: Dennis Walker/Giuseppe Baggi (Narrow box), Florence Temko (Wingding), Francis Ow (Modular cube), Guspath Go (Welsh corgi), Jeff Beynon (Sentinel bird), Marc Kirschenbaum (T-Rex), Martin Wall (Boat with keel), Nick Robinson/Mick Guy (Around the houses), Rene Lucio/Nick Robinson (Finger puppet), Robert Lang (Wild goat), Robin Glynn (Gift box), Ted Megrath (Pipe). The Banger, Basketball hoop, Butterfly, Crown, Fortune-teller, Ninja star, Penguin, Sailboat, Sanbow (Box with legs), Star box, Tulip, and Waterbomb are traditional in origin. The remainder of the designs are by Nick Robinson.

My thanks to: Wayne Brown for diligent proofreading, to Lewis Brown for computer repairs, to Sharon Turvey for loaning us her delicate hands and folding skills for the photo demonstrations, to my wife and children for making every effort to avoid origami at any cost. To my cats Matilda (alias Mogzilla) and Gomez, who turned 19 recently and isn't long for this world, to Nigel Molesworth for inspiration, to the Betty Black Band, Joe, and anyone who has endured, sorry, enjoyed my solo ambient gigs. To Loopers Delight and the Chain-Tape Collective. To whoever invented banana and orange fruit juice, to all my origami friends around the world, especially master-punter Ann Lavin, Master Kunihiko Kasahara, Brilly, Paulo & Silke, Kalmon and Thoki, Halle & Nicola Terry, Eric Grenouille, Mark Robinson (no relation) and Mark Bolitho, all at BOS, JOAS, MFPP, CDO, OUSA, AEP (origami societies). Finally, to all the staff at Quarto who helped make the book possible.

For more information about origami, try the following:

Author's website: www.origami.me.uk
United States: www.origami-usa.org
Canada: www.origami.vancouver.bc.ca
Britain: www.britishorigami.info
Australia: www.papercrane.org
New Zealand: jbax@mindspring.com
Singapore: www.geocities.com/albert_s.geo/SOW.htm

You can write to the British Origami Society membership secretary for details of joining—we have many hundreds of international members and always welcome new ones. Write to: 2a The Chestnuts, Countesthorpe, Leicester LE8 5TL, England